WITHDRAWN

THE TOWER OF BABEL

THE TOWER OF BABEL
Identity and Sanity

by

Adi Shmueli

HUMANITIES PRESS

Atlantic Highlands, N. J.

1978

Library of Congress Cataloging in Publication Data

Shmueli, Adi, 1941.
    The Tower of Babel.

    Bibliography: p.
    Includes index.
    1. Identity (Psychology) 2. Mental health.
3. Babel, Tower of. I. Title.
BF697.S52   155.2   77-13364
ISBN 0-391-00776-9

Printed in the United States of America

Acknowledgment

Thanks are due to Richard Huett for the work he invested in editing this book and for his talent for distinguishing between the essential and non-essential.

Thanks are also due to my wife, Iris, for her helpful comments and the atmosphere she provided which made the writing of this book possible.

To Alfred and Rivka with love

Contents

LIST OF ILLUSTRATIONS

Raphael: *Madonna of the Goldfinch*

Monet: *The Houses of Parliament, Sunset*

Picasso: *Les Demoiselles D'Avignon*

Picasso: *Daniel-Henry Kahnweiler*

Balla: *Dynamism of a Dog on a Leash*

Boccioni: *The City Rises*

Carrà: *Simultaneity—Woman on a Balcony*

Balla: *Swifts: Paths of Movement + Dynamic Sequences*

Kandinsky: *Improvisation #30*

Da Vinci: *Mona Lisa*

These illustrations appear, as a separate unit, between pages 48 and 49

xi

Sophistication and Soul Healing

What is the identity of man? What would be a sane self-image or a sane representation of the world? This book tries to show that sane and insane are elusive determinations. Sanity is as difficult to define as insanity and this is because *all* identities are elusive. The identities of people or other objects as we *experience* them are not solid entities eternally maintaining their sameness. A person, a chair, a table constantly change in our experience, and while changing they remain half-hidden, half-revealed, perennially playing the hide-and-seek game. The book strives to familiarize the reader with this shifting nature of all identities, including his own.

Not only psychologists have been trying to define sanity or determine the identity of man. Since the beginning of history man has been trying to form an image of the *real* world in contrast to what he considered unreal or imaginary. Philosophers, scientists and artists continue their pursuit for the true, authentic or sane representation of the universe or of the particular objects found in it. This book integrates psychology into a wider cultural context in which the artist, the philosopher or the religious man struggles to find and maintain a sane awareness of himself and of the world.

And the interest in the subject of identity is not only academic but also practical. In trying to help his patients, a psychotherapist must determine *what* troubles them, *where* these troubles come from and *how* to surmount them. In other words, he has to establish the *identity* of the patient's mental difficulty, its cause as well as its cure. But if indeed all identities are elusive, the therapist must constantly walk a tightrope. He might harm his patient by rushing into erroneous conclusions as to what is good or bad for him. On the other hand he might be threatened by the elusiveness of the patient's mental trouble and would then refrain from any statement. The elusiveness of man's nature and the uncertainty as to what precisely contributes to or impairs his mental wellbeing continue to be a baffling enigma with which every therapist nevertheless has to contend. Here, a comparison between contemporary psychotherapists and the ancient Sophists is relevant since modern knowledge about man is still relative, not markedly richer than what the Sophists knew about the nooks and crannies of the human soul.

The Sophists were wanderer educators who roamed among Greek cities but were concentrated in Athens in the 5th century B.C. Socrates befriended some of them. For adequate, sometimes exorbitant fees they would help people, especially the youth, acquire social skills and earthly wisdom so that they would become, as a modern therapist would say, "well adjusted" and prosperous. They would acquaint the young person with life's demands as well as pitfalls so that he would succeed in his career. Here are the words of Protagoras, an eminent Sophist:

> "Young man, if you associate with me, on the very first day you will return home a better man than you came, and better on the second day than on the first, and better every day than you were on the day before. . . . A teacher of this sort I believe myself to be, and above all other men to have the knowledge which makes a man noble and good."[1]

One could compare the Sophists to counseling psychologists who seek to orient their patients in life's demands and vicissitudes. They taught their clients practical know-how, public appeal and, most important, rhetoric. Rhetoric is the art of disputation, persuasion and discourse; it is the cultivation of the spoken and the written word. Their clients were trained to express themselves forcefully (assertive therapy) and elegantly outsmart any rival, be it a political opponent, a prosecutor in court or an overbearing father-in-law. Gorgias, another prominent Sophist, emphasized the magical power of words and recognized the fact that sophistry and rhetoric, apart from their tremendous value in achieving a career, also have a therapeutic effect on man. Words sooth and relieve, gladden and mould the soul. Protagoras compared sophistry to medicine inasmuch as the wise man achieves by means of the word what the doctor brings about by means of drugs.

Similar to most modern therapists, the Sophists were not religiously oriented and they had no religious principle to tell them *a priori* how they should guide their clients or judge their behaviors. "Concerning the gods," Protagoras said, "I cannot know either that they are or that they are not; for there are many obstacles to knowledge: the obscurity of the subject and the shortness of man's life." He added: "Man is the measure of all things."

Given the limits of human reason, the Sophists developed a keen sense for the relative in life. They knew what experienced therapists well know, namely that life has many aspects, one not absolutely better or absolutely worse than any other. They insisted that good and bad are relative terms: "Sickness," as one anonymous Sophist put it, "is bad for the sick, good for the physician. Death, bad for the dying, good for the undertakers and tomb makers."

But the awareness of the relative in life is double-faced: It can make a person humble and reserved but it can, on the other hand, generate dogmatic overconfidence, cynicism and dishonesty. Therefore, some Sophists were successful in their trade and were loved, others were subversive and were hated. Shunning pretensions to absolute knowledge, wise Sophists generally focused their attention on what is available for man in his short life span and were resourceful in helping their clients avoid pitfalls and to advance to excellence. However, whereas the first Sophists like Protagoras and Gorgias were concerned with culture and civic improvement, the later Sophists became more interested in their own inflated egos. They developed an opportunistic approach to life based on the fallacious argument that since everything is relative, whatever one says is right. They became jugglers of rhetoric, prepared to refute any argument, however true or false it might be.

This, naturally, detached Sophistry from its originally strong ties with real life and turned it into an abstract exercise in mental acrobatics which haughtily judged human values and behavior from above, or *ex cathedra*. For this alienation from life, the Sophists eventually paid a heavy price. The Athenians and the citizens of other cities in Greece came to hate them without distinguishing between wheat and chaff. Protagoras was exiled and his books were burnt in public. Rumors also claimed that he was later drowned in a ship that was sunk by an enemy. In their anger, the Athenians also associated Socrates with the less savory Sophists. This lover of wisdom, loved and admired by many, was tried and executed for "malpractice" i.e., impiety and corruption of the youth.[2]

This history of the Sophists presents a problem with which contemporary psychotherapists are confronted. Given the elusiveness of human identity, and the uncertainty as to what would support or harm human sanity, psychotherapists must be careful to avoid the pitfalls which destroyed the Sophists. In this book we present a model of a psychotherapist who helps his fellowmen while constantly contending with the elusiveness of all identities. We named this therapist the Babel therapist and we describe how he moulds identities in the minds of his patients as well as causing other identities to dissolve. He does this with the help of clear as well as ambiguous communications. And there is a major difference between him and the Sophists. Whereas the latter distanced themselves from real life and reveled in abstract gamesmanship, the Babel therapist remains immersed in life, acutely aware of its infinite complexity and his own limitations.

While writing this book, the author has tried to surmount the barrier of technical language which separates many readers from academic disciplines. He has therefore used some myths and parables to convey his ideas.

CHAPTER 1

The Sane People of Babel

Now the whole earth had one language and few words. And as men migrated from the east, they found a plain in the land of Shinar and settled there. And they said to one another, "Come, let us make bricks, and burn them thoroughly." And they had brick for stone, and bitumen for mortar. Then they said, "Come, let us build ourselves a city, and a tower with its top in the heavens, and let us make a name for ourselves, lest we be scattered abroad upon the face of the whole earth." And the Lord came down to see the city and the tower, which the sons of men had built. And the Lord said, "Behold, they are one people, and they have all one language; and this is only the beginning of what they will do; and nothing that they propose to do will now be impossible for them. Come, let us go down, and there confuse their language, that they may not understand one another's speech." So the Lord scattered them abroad from there over the face of all the earth and they left off building the city. Therefore its name was called Babel, because there the Lord confused the language of all the earth; and from there the Lord scattered them abroad over the face of the earth.

GENESIS 11.1-9

A human drama unfolds itself in this Biblical story about the Tower of Babel. We read about a group of people who embarked enthusiastically on a tremendous project—building a Tower—but failed to accomplish the task. Is this something that actually happened in the remote past?

The question is immaterial, as the Biblical myth is one of those stories that apply everywhere and in every generation although all the characters mentioned are fictitious. Essentially, the myth describes a *process of creation* through which all identities have always been formed. Human identity, that of various objects in the world or the identity of the entire universe develops in the same way. I am a Tower, you are a Tower, the table you write on is a Tower and, like an ancient forest, the universe contains nothing but an infinite number of Towers.

1

The people of Babel, we are told, were "men that migrated from the east." You can imagine the fears and anxieties that migrations or displacements always involve. What they dreaded most was the fleeting, precarious existence of nomads; they said: " . . . Let us make a name for ourselves, lest we be scattered abroad upon the face of the whole earth." They apparently came to the new place in small groups or as separate individuals and in seeking a *name* they craved for the unity of one nation that is rooted in clearly defined territory. As scattered individuals they were bound to perish not only from cold, hunger or thirst, but also from the lack of self-identity or, as they put it, the absence of a *name*.

A human being draws his identity from a group. You are what you are partly because you belong to this or that group of people. You speak their language, behave as they taught you to behave. You are French, English or a New Yorker with a Bronx accent. In each case your identity is determined in a social context. And it is this identity that the people of Babel sought in trying to find themselves a *name*. Their enterprise symbolizes a movement from a formless aggregate of elements to an organized and well integrated social unity. It is also a shift from ambiguity and lack of identity into the domain of meaning. For unless baptized and named, that is to say, related to a specific context, any existence would remain ambiguous and devoid of meaning.

But there is more to the myth. Along with the search for a *name* or identity, the people of Babel also started to erect a massive Tower. Any identity, whether that of a person or a group, requires a tangible mark and cannot remain abstract or only "in the mind" of its bearer. Without footprints of some sort, a concrete mark, a sound or a color, no identity can be spotted or established. Even ghosts need objective signs to announce their presence. They bang a shutter in the attic at night or make the wind whistle through the chimney. People, on the other hand, daily salute their visible reflections in the mirror, just to check that they are still there. They jealously guard other tangible marks of their identity, objects like badges, old pictures or souvenirs. And like individuals, societies and cultures coin their identities in objects like shrines, temples, flags, rituals, etc., which give concrete, visible dimensions to their values.

Identity needs a palpable mark not only to announce its presence but also to secure its continuity in time. We like to capture and preserve the child's fleeting smile in photographs. Societies preserve their identities in flags, altars or other concrete signs. Short of these signs, social systems would remain vulnerable to man's whims and vagaries which usually deprive them of duration or stability. Therefore, although created and consecrated by the spirit of a united society, a flag and a shrine, being concrete signs, soon become the guardians of this society, securing its historical continuity. This is why the people of Babel sought to eternalize their union in the massive solidity of a skyscraping Tower bearing their name. The huge edifice was meant to become the objective representation of their newly acquired identity which would make the latter last for many generations. After all, the identity of a society must survive the first generation that created it.

But the people of Babel were eventually forced to leave their city and abandon their half-accomplished or half-destroyed Tower. They came to the place to escape dispersion, nomadic life, ambiguous or undefined self-identity. Their unity towered itself above the earth, providing them with a new identity and meaningful existence. But soon they found themselves where they had first started; they dissolved into a human scatter. They sought eternal identity but found dispersion. It is believed that once they were forced to leave their city and thereby dissolve their unity, new languages and nations developed in the world. People started to move back and forth from diversity to unity. Symbolically, this refers to the developmental process of every identity.

Look at the lowest form of biological evolution, at a tiny creature like the slime mould. This is an amoeba which lives on bacteria found among decaying leaves in forests. It multiplies by simple cell division every few hours until the amoeba population reaches explosive proportions causing severe food shortages. At that point, the amoebas, to better their chances of survival, stop behaving as individuals and gather into groups which form clumps visible to the naked eye. These clumps "form straggling streamers of living matter, which . . . orient themselves towards central collection points. . . . At the hub of each central aggregation point, a mound begins to form as groups of amoebas mount themselves atop other groups. . . . This hub gradually rises first into the shape of a blunt peg, and then into a distinctly phallic erection. When all the incoming streams of amoebas are almost completely incorporated into this erected cartridge-like form, it topples onto its side, now looking like small, two-millimeters-long, slimy sausage. This slug begins now to migrate across the forest floor to a point where, hopefully, more favorable ecological conditions will prevail. . . . After migrating for a variable period of time (which can be two minutes or two weeks) in the direction of light and warmth, this slug . . . gradually erects itself once again into its phallic shape until it is standing on its tail. . . . This oval shape gradually assumes the form of a candle flame, bellied at the bottom and coming to a point at the top. . . . The end result is a delicate tapering shaft capped by a spherical mass of spores. When the spores are dispersed . . . each can split open to liberate a tiny new amoeba." [1]

All biological development shows this pendulum swing between unity and diversity. For Werner,[2] organismic development always proceeds from a state of relative globality to a state of increasing differentiation, articulation and hierarchical organization. And Piaget[3] showed how this swing between unity and diversity characterized the development of the child's cognitive powers. The infant's world is first described as diffuse unity. His perception is vague, lacking distinctive marks. But with development, the infant begins to see distinct images of the world surrounding him. He learns to differentiate between some colors and some shapes. However, at first the infant does not integrate the different images he sees into the unity of one object. For example, he does not think that the different colors he might encounter on a cube indeed belong to one and the same cube. It is only towards the end of his second year of life that the child acquires full awareness of object identity. But this identity, as we shall later see, is only relative. Piaget showed that the child's cognitive development is a dynamic process in which different levels of object identity are achieved, always followed or preceded by different levels of differentiation. In the human mind many Towers rise and fall.

Closely connected to this reference to biological and cognitive development is yet another aspect of the myth which evokes sexual imagery in the mind. The rising Tower of Babel could represent the process of sexual arousal in men and elevation of the clitoris accompanied with muscle tension in women. In both men and women, sexual arousal is a total response of the entire body involving increased muscle tension and generalized vasocongestion. In sexual intercourse both body and consciousness become immersed into a feeling of ultimate unity and a strict sense of self-assertion leading to a tight union with a sexual partner. However, love and intercourse are not solely a private affair. Although initiated by individual desires, they also serve the procreation of the human race. The unity of the couple soon turns into the diversity implied in the very act of procreation. At the consummation of intercourse, the penis ejaculates numerous sperms capable of forming new lives. And this ejaculation occurs through successive contractions of the penis which spurts out the sperms intermittently while shrinking. Similarly, the orgasm in women, reached at the peak of pelvic tension and vessel congestion, involves regularly recurring and rhythmical contractions of the uterus and the outer third of the vagina, both facilitating the passage of the sperms to the ovary. Thus, in both men and women orgasm is reached through backward movement or receding muscle contractions leading to the eventual creation of new lives. Similarly, it was the shrinkage and eventual demolition of the Tower of Babel that marked the dispersion of its builders and the creation of a new diversity of individuals, capable of forming new languages and new nations.

But why was the Tower destroyed? The development of a new national identity ended in dispersion. Symbolically, the Biblical myth refers to the fact that the birth of any identity is an aggressive act, very likely to be punished or thwarted. The new always aggresses against the old or against whatever lies outside its fresh boundaries. So we see an external factor—God—attacking the newly created unity of the people of Babel from the outside. The development of identity is never free of conflict.

The erection of the Tower was considered a flagrant challenge to God, an outrageous attempt to rival his might. "And the Lord said, behold, they are one people, and they have all one language; and this is only the beginning of what they will do; and nothing they propose to do will now be impossible for them." The Tower was deemed an obvious demonstration of power and independence; God was angered and he dispersed its builders. By its colossal dimensions, it dwarfed and overshadowed the surrounding hills and mountains; a human creation belittled God's creation. God's action was therefore a preemptive move aimed at a potential aggressor.

This clash between God and man is but a symbol of the inevitable conflict through which any identity is born and formed. Earlier we said that we acquire our identity from the group to which we belong, that a person is French or English because he shares characteristics of these people. But this is only partly true, for we are aware of our identity only to the extent that it *differs* from another identity. We notice our strength, wisdom and wealth *in comparison with or in contrast to* the weakness or frailty of others. When one identity asserts itself, it relegates other identities to the background. The birth of identity is therefore an aggressive act. Heracleitos was probably the first philosopher to understand that identities emerge through strife. And philosophers like Hegel, Marx and Sartre built their entire theories on this conflict among identities.

When we say that the creation of identity entails strife and aggression, we should distinguish between a negative and a positive aspect of aggression, both being implied in the colossal project of Babel. Most commonly, aggression connotes a negative act of encroachment, destruction or death. In this sense, an aggressive act does harm to someone. It destroys or at least disrupts an existing order in the world, turning a positive something into a virtual nothing. And this is precisely what the people of Babel were likely to do. Assured by their newly acquired unity and strength, they were deemed likely to abuse their power and impose themselves on their neighbors, if not on the whole world.

On the other hand, aggression can be positive as well as negative; it can involve creation and growth, not only destruction. After all, the project of Babel bears the signs of a creative or procreative act: A unity was added to the world, a new nation was born. The Tower constituted a new form, a huge structure imposing itself on the environment, proudly dominating the horizon and displaying the power of its architects. And in this sense, every imposition of form on matter, of structure on a chaos is an evidence of positive aggression which is commonly manifested in artistic activities, in scientific discoveries or any creation. The scientific mind literally imposes forms and structures on what was initially a meaningless jumble of unrelated phenomena. Also, the artist shapes formless matter into a variety of forms. A painter picks different colors and spreads them on the canvas. He arranges the colors—which are in themselves formless—in what he considers the "right" configuration. But the colors often are recalcitrant and the painter has to repeat his attempt to paint the "right" picture until he reaches— if at all—the moment when he says "that's it!" To achieve this artistic goal, the painter must demonstrate positive aggression. He has to muster his imaginative strength, concentrate his physical energy and achieve a unity of mind and body which would impose on the colors—through the movement of his hands—the desired configuration. This concentration of energy, responsible for the creation of new forms, is not different from the strength that was required to erect the colossal Tower of Babel. In each case, despite the resistance of formless matter or any other destructive or opposing force, a new identity survived "birth pangs" and came into existence.

But it is not easy to determine when positive aggression starts and when negative aggression ends. These two aspects of aggression are tightly related to one another. Creation and destruction often result from one and the same act. Psychologists and biologists have long been debating the causes of aggressive behavior in man but their opinions on this matter vary and the issue remains controversial. Freud concentrated on the destructive behavior of man (i.e. on negative aggression) and he believed that the urge to destroy is an innate drive linked to an intrinsic death wish we all assumingly harbor in ourselves. But other theorists[4] contest this view, claiming that negative aggression is not inherent in man's nature but is only a learned behavior, a habit one can in principle discard or "unlearn." Ethologists, on the other hand, have stressed the positive rather than the negative aspect of aggression and have considered positive aggression a spontaneous, in-born response in the organism, which safeguards the survival of the species.[5] Thus Lorenz[6] and Storr[7] point to the association between aggression and sexual behavior and emphasize their instinctive nature. Aggression is needed for the procreation and the survival of the species. For example, genital display and penis erection by monkeys, besides being a prelude to sexual intercourse, also serve to ward off an invading stranger.[8] In erecting his penis, the male primate asserts its rights over its territory and threatens the invading stranger with immediate attack. The strong male monkey in the herd periodically mounts male monkeys of weaker position in the social hierarchy in order to recon-firm his own position as the leader. In some human societies penis erection, either symbolical or actual, is meant to assert one's power or to ward off spirits and demons.[9] However, it is easy to see how these examples of positive aggression commonly involve negative aggression in the form of an assault or killing. It is then difficult to separate the two aspects of aggression. The positive aggression that preserves a species is at the same time a negative aggression addressed against another species, involving killing and death.

As to the human species, survival and self-preserving activities have yet another meaning which does not apply to other species. Like other animals, man has to protect his physical existence and secure his survival. But man is a thinking animal and his survival does not involve only physical preservation but also identity conservation. In fact, one could kill a person without thereby destroying his identity. The dead people could still be remembered for what they were and their physical death would not necessarily alter their identity. As we shall stress in the following chapters, man's existence is not only a biological fact but also a spiritual identity characterized by a set of beliefs about himself and about his world. It is this spiritual identity that gives meaning to his existence, and the introduction of new meaning or new beliefs into his life would necessarily threaten his existence. And many people would prefer physical death to loss of identity or traditional values. Therefore, in the human world negative aggression might appear not only as a physical act like beating or strangling but also as a subtle communication that shakes the person's identity and therefore threatens his existence.

But, again, self-identity or self-definition is born and preserved only *in contrast to, in relation to* or *at the expense of* another identity. Human identity is never born in the wilderness or in a social vacuum but always in a world populated with various identities. Therefore, if a person adopts a certain self-definition or identity he thereby also rejects another identity. For example, he who asserts himself as a saint would at the same time disassociate himself from evil and its advocates. In this sense, sainthood contrasts itself with evil qualities and rejects them. Positive self-assertion entails negation of other identities, which is likely to lead to an open conflict for survival. Once we become aware of the contrast that any self-identity implies, the question as to the causes of human aggression can be seen in a different light. Let us assume that our planet suffers from no material scarcity that would threaten man's existence so that no person would need to kill or learn other aggressive behaviors to safeguard his survival. Let us pretend that this world is infinite and that every person can find enough space and nutrition for himself. Still, this hypothetical condition would not eliminate conflicts and aggression from the world. For if the human mind indeed always conceives of identities in relation to other identities, then man's awareness of this world is not free from conflict. We should recall Heracleitos' belief that reality is an eternal strife between opposites, for example, between night and day, warm and cold, etc. In the following chapters we will show that by virtue of the contrast among identities, every single identity constantly threatens and is in turn threatened by other identities.

And it is this contrast among identities and the mixture between positive and negative aggression that the Biblical myth conveys. In searching for a *name,* the people of Babel assumed self-responsibility in finding meaning for their existence and thereby creating their own identity. But this act also meant rejecting God who is assumed, in a religious context, to be the originator of meaning and the creator of all identities. This was then a titanic struggle with God for the power of creation or for the identity of a Creator. In piercing the skies high above, the erected Tower diffused, with its colossal dimensions, an air of self-sufficiency and self-creation. And, obviously, this clash of identities was also a fight for control over the world. For he who provides structure, meaning and identity to any situation also controls it. Identity conflict implies power conflict. The way the people of Babel were punished indicates that identity conflict was indeed the issue. God did not exterminate them physically but confused their language so "that they may not understand one another's speech." In other words, God deprived them of the means of communication essential for the creation and maintenance of meaning, unity and identity. And God reacted in this way out of fear of what the new unity of the people of Babel might do. The birth and survival of a new national unity— positive aggression—also involved a threat for some other existing order which was, in this case, God's control of the world and the meaning He gives to it. In a later chapter we will see that the same pattern of identity conflict also characterizes human relationships.

But was this identity conflict between man and God the only reason that thwarted the completion of the Tower? Was it only an external factor—God—that baffled the quest for identity and dissolved the nascent unity of the people of Babel? Does not the Biblical myth suggest the possibility that internal factors within the newly born people were equally opposed to the completion of the Tower and the consolidation of the unity it symbolized? Contradictory though it may seem, the people of Babel were on the one hand eager to build their Tower but on the other hand reluctant to witness the complete achievement of this goal.

The Biblical myth only mentions the desire of the people of Babel for a *name* and unity but does not specify the name that they actually chose for themselves. The name "Babel" was given to the city by an

external observer or a historian who described the episode a long
time after its actual occurrence. The name is derived from the Hebrew
verb, "balbel," which means to confuse. History designated and remembered the episode of the Tower by its eventual outcome, namely,
the confusion that God inflicted on the people that built it. But this
is not their name. The Biblical story does not mention the real name
of these people and the absence of this name is not an accidental
omission or negligence on the part of the historian who wrote the myth.
The name is absent because the people that sought to acquire a name
were also reluctant to choose a specific one. From one point of view
we can say that at the end their Tower was left partly "destroyed,"
thereby referring to the intervention of an external factor thwarting
the enterprise. But from another point of view one can say that the
Tower was left only partly "accomplished" because the people themselves recoiled just before the final completion of their project. They
actively avoided the final result despite their marked eagerness to
build the Tower. And this is not, as we shall progressively realize, a
testimonial to their "success neurosis" or "castration complex" as a
psychoanalyst would claim, but rather a universal characteristic of
identity which on the one hand seeks and on the other hand evades
final and well established definitions.

When we entertain intimate relationships with people, we commonly interact with them without constantly labeling or defining their
nature. In fact, the more we label a person the more we distance ourselves from him. It is when husband and wife cease to love one another
and divorce that they exchange the maximum number of labels and
constantly define each other's identity. But when they love one another,
they tend to interact, implicitly reflecting their qualities in their daily
relationship but seldom attaching to them fixed labels. And similar
to them, the people of Babel shunned final self-definition. Because
a label or a final self-definition would mean a stultified existence and
an arrest of human growth, a stagnation or death. In a sense, only
the dead people possess completed and fixed identities since they
are no more capable of redefining themselves. The people of Babel
searched for identity but they also dreaded its final acquisition which
resembles in many ways the finality of death. As long as they were
absorbed in their project they refrained from the attainment of a final
identity although they were constantly striving for it. We can imagine
them defining and redefining the meaning of their unity, enacting and

then amending social laws, specifying and then changing daily goals. Being alive, they wished to retain a good portion of existential ambiguity and actively resisted fixed norms or unchangeable names. It is only after they had been dispersed that a name was given to their unity. But by then that people no longer existed.

Thus, the disintegration of the unity of the people of Babel represents not only the conflict with an external force—God—but also man's attraction to ambiguity and his own resistance to fixed unities or identities. The half-accomplished or half-destroyed Tower that the people of Babel left behind constitutes a visual symbol of what man can achieve in a life span. He longs for absolute and eternal identity but would accept only partial definitions of himself, only half identity or a fragment of the truth so that he could feel alive and capable of redefining himself. This means that self-identity and, as we shall see, any identity, would always remain half-hidden, half-revealed, constantly appearing and disappearing, on the one hand crystallizing through the use of a *name* and on the other hand losing its unity by transcending the limits of labels and definitions.

The story of the Tower symbolically recapitulates this perennial process in which identity develops while steering in different directions and assuming opposing meanings. We said that the building of the Tower and its subsequent downfall represent pendulum swings between unity and diversity, meaning and ambiguity, both being conveyed also by the sexual connotations of the symbolism used. Sexual arousal and procreation are repeated oscillations between union and separation, unity and diversity. We also said that the birth of identity is, like any act of creation, an aggressive act, both in the negative and the positive sense of the term. As a symbol, the half-accomplished and half-destroyed Tower would refer to identity as being a *process,* not a static entity. Any identity would resemble an image which is constantly formed yet never accomplished. Identities are entities that always remain elusive as they perennially play a game which one can appropriately call the *existential yo-yo game.*

Note that in the yo-yo game, the downgrade movement of the ball is at the same time an accumulation of energy which later pulls the ball upward. The descent of the ball would stand for separation and differentiation whereas its ascent would be the return to unity and integration. These opposing movements, or the yo-yo game, characterize the development of all identities, whether the identities of objects which develop in the human mind, the identity of the universe as it is conceived by man or the identity of a social structure as it is expressed by its political form. An example of the last identity would reveal this yo-yo movement.

In the 19th century, romantic ideas swept Europe and found expressions in philosophy, religion, art as well as in the political movements of that time. Romanticism in politics found one expression in the anarchist movement. Being inflamed by the romantic movement, the anarchists hated the traditional political structure of society, namely the *state,* and they tried to destroy it. They considered the state an obsolete form of government imposed on individuals, alienating their rights and stifling their growth and creativity. In contrast to the drab uniformity implied by the term "citizen" which the state forces on its people, the anarchists emphasized the freedom of the individual, his uniqueness and creativity. However, this emphasis on the individual and the attempt to tear him free from the unity of the state (downgrade yo-yo movement) were simultaneously counterbalanced by new visions of political structures—a unified society of workers—which would replace the state. One political identity or Tower is hardly dismantled before another one starts to rise. Proudhon, Sorel and Bakunin cherished a variety of political visions about a presumably true and "organic" unity of all workers in one country as well as across all countries. But then a question was raised as to whether the individual they esteemed so much could indeed survive in a surging *élan* of a revolutionary movement or in a colossal union of all workers across all nations. Many studies have shown how totalitarianism in politics has deep roots in romantic aspirations.[10] While fighting the state in the name of the individual and his freedom, many anarchists were at the same time dreaming of new social orders exceeding the state in proportions and very likely to engulf the individual completely. But when this happens, as is the case in countries that have experienced socialist revolutions, people again start to think about the freedom of the individual in relation to the existing political structure.

This historical example reminds us that the identity of the best political structure that would adequately reconcile the freedom of the individual with society has not yet received its final definition. People will continue to unite and separate in the typical yo-yo movement as they try to create their social and political identity. And this yo-yo movement characterizes, as we shall see, the development of all identities, whether social or individual.

Having dealt with the elusiveness of all identities, we are now to define sanity and insanity. Obviously, the concepts of sanity and identity are interrelated; don't we speak of the insane person as "not being *himself*"? On the one hand insanity is the lack of identity, cohesion or unity. It is a state of mind containing a pell-mell of unrelated thoughts and unstable feeling, a spiritual dispersion resembling the people of Babel before they decided to unite—a multiplicity of individuals about to be scattered "upon the face of the whole earth." But on the other hand, insanity is also equivalent to the possession of a fixed existence or identity rigidly defined by specific *names* which the people of Babel were wise to avoid. Insane is he who freezes his being in one identity, he who likes to repeat constantly that "two and two are four" and that people should be or do *only* this and that and nothing else. Insanity, therefore, consists not only in not having a name but also in having a specific one. And what is sanity? It is not a state but a process, a dynamic change and not a fixed condition. Sanity is the existential yo-yo game in which all identities remain elusive, constantly in the making yet never accomplished.

In the following chapters, we want to show that sanity can be learned, that a person can, like the people of Babel, be educated to develop an elusive and therefore healthy identity.

CHAPTER 2

The Formation of Identity

In this chapter we will study the way in which awareness of identities forms in the human mind. We will see that this formation is a continuous cognitive process. The terms "cognitive" and "cognition" which we often use in this book are not restricted to the abstract thinking of the mind but cover all mental activities whether they involve abstract symbols, linguistic concepts or simple imagery.

The word "identity" could be confusing as it has two different connotations. There is first the identity we perceive, experience, live, and then there is also the identity we talk about. The latter belongs to language, whereas the former is part of life. There is obviously a big difference between, for example, actually looking at a woman and merely speaking later about her. In this book, the term "identity" will refer to the actual experience we have of identities, not to identities we only speak or communicate about. However, people tend to confuse the two and we should therefore clarify the difference.

If one wants to talk to a friend and be understood, he must speak in a logical way. And logic emphasizes the concept of identity. In a trial, each time the prosecutor, the attorney for the defense or the judge speak about the defendant, it is assumed that they talk about the same person, or else the consequences could be grave. Whenever you talk about your wife to someone and this person nods his head understandingly, it is again assumed that you both speak about the same woman. Without the concept of identity, communication would be impossible.

But logic applies only to the way we construct sentences and talk to people. Both logic and language are something abstract that does not adequately reflect the manner we actually perceive or experience the world. Language has nouns like "chair," "table," "man" and "donkey." Each word, each noun sounds like an independent unit, surely

14

complete and sufficient to itself. And most people commonly confuse linguistic nouns with reality itself, believing that nouns stand for real objects that always remain identical to themselves. It is as if objects were eternal. We believe, for example, that the car we presently drive is identical with the car we drove yesterday. We are certain we are the identical person we were last week or last month. Often, the presumably *real* self-sameness becomes a value to be attained. People might address a person and say: "Be authentic, be your-self," assuming that the person knows what his *real* self is. But only words are identical to themselves. Identity, in the sense of actual experience, is never a given object that remains identical with itself while, so to speak, it is "lying there" in the world. It is rather a process in which different levels of identity awareness are formed.

Whereas a linguistic noun like "chair" appears as a complete unit, separate from other nouns, actual perception always contains duality or relation. You can never see only one thing, you always see two things—a figure and a background that enter into complex relations. Take a pencil and put a dot on a white sheet. Try to focus your eyes only on the dot all the time. You cannot! Your eyes constantly shift from the black dot to the white background and vice versa. What you perceive is actually a dynamic relation between two factors, not a single and static unit. Also the chair we actually observe in the kitchen never appears isolated. It always relates to the floor, the table, the walls or to someone sitting on it. The things we perceive in the world are much more "sociable" than we tend to admit. Only the word "chair" appears separate and remains identical to itself; the chair we actually see is never the same chair. Each time we look at it, different levels of identity awareness are formed in our mind. In these levels of awareness, we tend to organize the stimuli we perceive in configurations we commonly call "objects," "men," "women," etc. But these actually perceived or experienced objects never possess absolute or real identity. Like the Tower of Babel, they tend to rise and fall in our minds, consolidate and dissolve, and their identity is nothing but a process of formation which is never completed. In this process a *relative* sameness or permanence of objects is achieved. After all, we do have a relatively clear idea of how our car looks and we know how to identify it every morning. But this relatively permanent identity of the car or of other objects is only temporary and incomplete. Now, how does this identity awareness form?

Every morning I am able to identify my car in the parking lot because in my mind I carry a condensed image or representation which highlights its shape, its different colors, location and so on. It is as if I carried the car in my mind, conserving its identity by the use of images. Similarly, with a sign like the three letter word "Jim" we retain in our mind the identity of a person we know and a red mark on a door might refer to a specific danger. Identity awareness starts to crystallize with the use of symbolic *signifiers* like an image, a name, linguistic signs and marks of all kinds. A symbolic signifier is the carrier of identity and without it identity would not be perceived or experienced. Piaget showed that the child acquires awareness of relatively permanent objects only towards the end of the second year of life when his symbolic imagery develops.[1]

In studying the stages of cognitive development in children, Piaget showed that there are different levels of identity awareness that children attain as they grow up. From birth to adolescence there are different intellectual stages through which the child passes as he matures. And in each successives stage his mind has a different, qualitatively more developed awareness of object identity. One common denominator, however, characterizes identity awareness in all stages. Intellectual development and, concomitantly, the child's cognitive awareness of identities swing from stages of organized unity towards plurality of representations and again to articulate unity and so forth. It is as if the child's mind constantly relives the story of Babel.

In the early months of the first year of life the child does not possess a unified representation of an object and is therefore unaware of object permanence or identity. At this stage of cognitive development, the child's perception is fragmentary and he sees objects as a plurality of discrete or separate images. For example, a seven-month-old child would play with an object as he sees it in the same spot, always present before his eyes. Once this object is removed or hidden behind a screen the child would not look for it, certainly believing that object ceased to exist. In the eyes of a child, the object changes its identity once it changes its position in space. Describing an experiment conducted with his daughter, Jacqueline, age seven months, Piaget writes:

> Jacqueline tries to grasp a celluloid duck on top of her quilt. She almost catches it, shakes herself, and the duck slides down beside her. It falls very close to her hand but behind

a fold in the sheet. Jacqueline's eyes have followed the movement. . . . But as soon as the duck has disappeared—
nothing more! It does not occur to her to search behind the
fold of the sheet . . . I then take the duck from its hiding
place and place it near her hand three times. All three times
she tries to grasp it, but when she is about to touch it I replace
it very obviously under the sheet. Jacqueline immediately
withdraws her hand and gives up. The second and third times
I make her grasp the duck through the sheet and she shakes
it for a brief moment but it does not occur to her to raise
the cloth.[2]

For Jacqueline the duck exists only as a plurality of images such
as "the duck under the sheet," "the duck under the table," "the duck in
front of the eye." These images are as yet uncoordinated and unrelated;
Jacqueline believes she sees different dolls each time the doll appears.
It is only throughout the second year of life that the child progressively
acquires an awareness of object identity as it is demonstrated in her
attempt to look for hidden objects. The child will continue to look for
the ball after it disappears under the bed or under the pillow. The
changes in position, which she previously considered disparate images
of different objects, have now become the attributes of the same object
which can be hidden under the sheet, under the table, being here, there,
etc. Whereas in earlier months the child was capable only of recording
successive or sequential appearences of the object without seeing their
inherent unity, now the child has become capable of simultaneously
grasping the different spatial positions of the object and relating them
to the same unity of the object. Identity is born once a multiplicity
of different perspectives become simultaneously coordinated and related
into one unity. Hide the ball, throw it under the table or put it on the
sofa, the two-year-old child will always consider it the same. At this
age the child also develops symbolic imagery and is capable of using
this awareness of object permanence to develop elementary processes
of problem solving. For example, at 16 months of age, Piaget's son,
Laurent, used a stick to obtain a toy that otherwise was out of reach,
although he had never used a stick in this way before.

However, this identity awareness on the part of the two-year-old
child is only relative. Compared with the fragmentary or sequential
perception of images characteristic of earlier months of life, the cog-

nition of the two-year-old child indeed demonstrates awareness of object unity within the plurality of its images. But when compared to subsequent stages of cognitive development, the identity awareness of this stage appears to be rather rudimentary and primitive in nature.

More specifically, when a two-year-old child plays with a ball and follows it wherever it rolls, he demonstrates in action a certain level of identity awareness: It is always the same ball he is looking for. However, this child cannot grasp other aspects of the object's identity besides its ability to remain the same while changing positions. The conservation of quantity is another aspect of object identity which the young child cannot grasp until he becomes seven or eight years of age. If you present two identical tall and thin containers filled with water to a four-year-old child, he will admit that they contain identical quantities of liquid. But, as Piaget showed in his famous experiment, the child will deny that the quantities are identical if the contents of one of these containers is poured, before his eyes, into a short, broad jar. The child will insist that the amount of water in the tall container is greater than the amount of water in the other.

In the words of Piaget, the child *centers* his attention only on a single, striking feature of the object—the height of the first container—and says that it contains more liquid because it is taller. He fails to *decenter* and consider both width and height simultaneously, thereby grasping that the height of one container is compensated by the width of the second. In other world, to *decenter* is to take into account, in a simultaneous way, different and complementary features of the object, in this case the width and the height of the containers. Centering on only one feature of the object, the child erroneously comes to the conclusion that: tall = big = more liquid. It is only at the age of seven or eight that identity awareness of quantity or, in other words, the awareness that water conserves its volume regardless of the shape of the jar in which it is poured, is achieved. Essentially, this identity awareness of quantity is attained when the child understands the notion of reversibility. The older child will say, "The water in the broad jar is the same because you can pour the water back to the tall container and then the height will be the same." He has therefore become aware of the reverse operation that will restore the original situation. Also, the child at this age develops identity awareness of weight as well as of classes. The preschool child does not understand the nature of classes and would, for example, regard every snail he sees as a separate instance of "snail." He does not understand, as an eight-year-old boy would, that each snail is a member of the class of snails, having identical or common characteristics of other snails.

Thus, in each stage of cognitive development, identity aware-ness is being formed by the ability to grasp simultaneously different aspects of the object or to apprehend the unity of the object within the plurality of its facets. When the child centers only on one single aspect of an object, ignoring other, equally important features, he displays what Piaget calls egocentrism. The egocentric mind sees the world only from a single point of view—its own—and is blind to other perspectives of reality. Obviously, an egocentric mind is rigid, un-adaptive and, in the long run, dangerous to the very survival of the person. To be blind to important features of reality is to run the risk of being labeled "insane" as well as to invite fatal blunders. We forgive the mistakes of young age and we call them "childish," not "insane." But from adults we expect more developed identity awareness. Ideally, we would want the human mind to be aware of all possible features of any object, at once conscious of all points of view of each matter, thereby shedding *all* residues of egocentrism. But is this possible? No. Man's identity awareness always retains a considerable degree of blindness, egocentrism or "insanity."

What is it we really see when we look at an object? One would think that painters could easily answer this question as they possess sensitive eyes. But then when one studies the history of art and looks at paintings from different schools, the question as to what the human eyes commonly see appears difficult to answer. Paintings as well as other products of human creativity are testimonials to two contradictory features, two opposite movements in the human mind. On the one hand, identities are perceived as relatively well crystallized, but, on the other hand they appear fleeting and nebulous, marked by fluidity and diversity. On the one hand, the mind feels it has a "solid" grip on "real" objects, but, on the other hand, these objects seem to dissolve as if the mind were not awake but in a dream. These two poles of human cognition have been described by artists and philosophers as the *classic* and the *romantic* tendencies of the mind. At the classic pole you will find presumably well-formed identities, but at the romantic pole, nebulosity reigns supreme. Between these two poles, the human mind has constantly been scurrying in constant search for the "true" object identity as well as the sense of sanity.

For the artist in ancient Greece, the "real" identity of objects did not reside in their appearances. When he looked at the visible world he was struck by the quick changes and the fleeting nature of all things seen. Birth and death, day and night, the hot and cold seasons—all these changes made the Greek artist dislike the visible world. He felt his goal was to paint *beauty* and *reality* and these could not reside in transient appearances subject to decay and death. However, behind the appearances of all objects there exist, so he believed, their ideal, pure, perfect and eternal *forms*. In other words, only the "true" identities, the pure forms of objects were considered beautiful and the goal of the artist was to represent in his work only these pure forms, not transient appearances. This emphasis on a presumably ideal form of an object, or the belief that such a form or identity indeed exists, is a major characteristic of the classical tendency in art and, more generally, in the human mind.

To take an example, wrinkles on the face of a woman result from the process of aging affecting all mortals. The classical artist would therefore feel the urge to purge the painted face of a woman of all wrinkles as he would think that they do not belong to the pure, ideal and eternal form of a woman's face. The paintings of Raphael are good examples of this early Hellenic ideal of art as it was revived in the Renaissance.

Take his painting *The Madonna of the Goldfinch*. The clarity and nobility of forms are striking. It is a purified, an ideal representation of faces, bodies, trees, etc. Also striking is the architectonic structure of the painting and its geometrical perfection. The three figures are firmly linked in an isosceles triangle and all other objects are perfectly arranged in perspective. The geometrical harmony is further stressed by the landscape in the background where two delicate trees balance the picture from each side. In fact, the geometrical proportions of the background make it a visible portion of a sphere that perfectly encircles the figures as its center and goes far beyond the edges of the canvas. The painting represents a unified and focused world with a clear center and harmoniously balanced periphery transfused with serenity, stability and emotional security.

The three figures occupy a central position in the painting. This is a major characteristic of classic art—the main theme or the main object painted is to occupy the center of the painting and less important objects are relegated to the periphery.[3] We said earlier that identities are born at the expense of other identities and the painting shows this conflict. There is an obvious imbalance between figure and background, the former clearly asserting itself against the latter. This is consistent with a major classic belief that the center is a position where the most perfect and most objective reality lies. Believing that this figure represents the most ideal and therefore "real" form, the classic painter tends to place it in the center of his painting.

But is this classic ideal in any sense close to reality? Critics of the classic school of art did not spare words to denigrate its ideal. It was rightly claimed that pure forms of objects are but abstractions with no basis in reality. Classic figures were therefore considered illusory, stilted, artificial, false, lacking substance and life, etc. Pure forms simply do not exist except in the imagination of the painter. Classic artists never reached a consensus regarding any specific object identity or ideal form and every artist saw these presumably ideal forms in his own specific way. No one could actually discover the "real" figure of a woman, a man or a horse. In fact, the search for the pure, ideal and eternal form of beauty could have brought art to stagnation and lack of variety, had it not been for the fact that artists indeed conceived the ideal form of beauty in different ways. Imagine what would have been the fate of art had the Greek artists indeed agreed upon the ideal and perfect form of a woman's face! The artistic representation of this face could only have been an empty geometrical abstraction bearing the least resemblance to human faces.

Furthermore, although believing they were representing ideal and presumably objective reality which is free from the transience of the visible world, the classic artists in Greece often knowingly tinted their products with subjective norms belonging to this finite and ephemeral universe. They were aware of the foreshortening characteristics of the normal conditions of vision.[4] For example, if you look at people from above, they will appear smaller and less impressive. On the other hand, sculptures placed high above eye level would appear to the beholder taller than what they are. Therefore, depending on the future positioning of a painting or a statue, the classic artist compensated for this foreshortening by a deliberate departure from the correct proportions of the object represented. Thus, despite his belief that ideal forms or "objective" identities exist, the classic artist could not adequately represent them. He was aware of the fact that, after all, reality is not totally "objective," that it depends on the position of the beholder and is continuously construed by his subjective impressions.

However, despite the elusiveness of "objective" reality, painters as well as people in general have always believed that it indeed exists. But what is it? What is the identity of the object seen? The critics of classic art generally pointed to the fact that the emphasis on the forms of objects is but a poor rendition of reality since it ignores many other facets of the perceived object. To use Piaget's terminology, the critics accused classic art of egocentrism of representation i.e., concentration only on one point of view of the objects—the frontal view—while neglecting other, equally important points of view. In general, those who departed from the Hellenic ideal of beauty sought to restore to objects the variety of forms or colors in which they reveal themselves to the perceiver. But the dissenters were divided as to what constitute the "true" or richest perception of an object.

The Impressionists, to take one example, were particularly attentive to the color sensations apprehended by the retina, to the variety of hues to which the classic artists were blind. They showed that the classic vision of nature is false and that once we adopt a new way of perceiving—to see with a virgin eye—a new richness of color would reveal itself. Indeed, one of the notable discoveries of Impressionism is the fact that shadows are not black; most often they appear tinted with different hues. By attempting to paint the objects exactly as they saw them, the Impressionists believed they were representing on their canvas the true identity of the object seen, namely, the richness and brilliance of its colors.

However, in laying emphasis on and carefully recording colors, the Impressionists often neglected the form of objects. Despite their conviction that they were representing the "real" experience we usually have of an object, they in fact distorted reality by sacrificing the forms of the objects seen. In the painting of Monet, Pissarro, Renoir and other Impressionists, the object often loses its solidity, as if it dissolves in the scintillation or blends of the colors used. And once again, painters had to raise the question as to the "true" identity of the object seen.

Cézanne tried to strike a new balance between color and form, thereby tackling problems that later became the focus of Cubism. And the issue was not only limited to the retrieval of a balance between form and color but also concerned a method of rendering volumes on a flat canvas. Objects in nature have volume which neither classic art nor Impressionism could represent. In finding the technical solution for this problem, the Cubist artist believed he succeeded in capturing and representing the "real" identity of the object perceived.

In 1907, Picasso finished his painting called *Les Demoiselles D'Avignon* which was to become a landmark in the history of art. What Picasso was aiming at was not different from the old classic goal, namely, to get back to the *durable* form of the thing seen by eliminating all irrelevant details.[5] Viewing volume as the basic characteristic of object identity, the problem was how to make this element perceptible on canvas. To achieve this goal, Picasso, Braque and other painters of this movement were careful to record on the canvas a group of simultaneous aspects particularly representative of the object in question. It is as if the eyes of the painter roamed around the object and simultaneously perceived its vertical, cross-section and horizontal facets. We should recall in this respect Piaget's emphasis on the coordination of multiple dimensions as being essential to the awareness of object permanence or object identity. The ideal in Cubism was essentially the same: to represent on the canvas multiple aspects of the object. Of course, the representation of these aspects is not a simple juxtaposition of successive angles of the object seen; the multiple points of view are fused into a single, more or less coherent image. Every figure in Picasso's *Les Demoiselles* represents this kind of fusion to a certain degree. And especially striking is the seated figure on the right. Here the volume is particularly pronounced as the frontal, profile and cross-section viewpoints are condensed into a single representation. Striking is also the impression of density and weight that pervades the painting. The figures are separated not by an empty space, but by almost palpable folds of curtains that tie the picture together into one unity.

To the Cubist artist, then, Raphael's paintings or classic art in general would appear almost as an "insane" distortion of reality because of the emphasis on the object's single or frontal point of view. The Cubist artist believes that, in contrast, his paintings have achieved a more complete representation of the object's identity as the latter is being considered from a multiplicity of angles. Ironically, however, the very attempt to capture the object's identity through its different points of view eventually brought its disintegration and made many Cubist paintings illegible. Picasso's *Les Demoiselles* was but the beginning of this artistic trend which sought to grasp object identity in the multiplicity of its perspectives. Soon Cubism tried to free the object or its volume from all perspectives; it is as if the dependence on actual perspectives, numerous as they may be, detracted from the true identity of the object.

For example, in the portrait of *Daniel-Henry Kahnweiler,* Picasso detached many planes from the volumes and presented them in front view. The solid volume of the head still exists, but only in implication since the planes of which it is composed have been abstracted and moved to the picture's surface. It is an attempt to represent a figure freed from objective perspectives, since each single perspective usually hides more than it reveals when one focuses on it separately. It is presumably a total liberation from one-sidedness or egocentrism. The painter tries to offer almost all the facets of the figure at once. A two-dimensional canvas is supposed to display a multi-dimensional experience of a beholder who would see the figure simultaneously from an infinite number of angles. However, this ambitious goal on the part of the painter made the painting far less legible than the *Les Demoiselles.* In the very attempt to provide a unified representation of all perspectives, the solid volumes of the head and the body almost dissolve. A reference to another, yet related, school of art would provide another example of how the identity of the object dissolves into a multiplicity of facets and this despite the avowed intention of the artist to represent its true cohesion and unity.

In the first decade of the twentieth century a group of Italian artists formed a new movement in art which they called Futurism. Although in many respects close to the Cubists, the Futurists saw their originality in their attempt to represent movement and speed in their artistic creation. They felt that the Cubists' attempt to represent volume, despite its obvious novelty, falls short of being a "true" representation of object identity since it is motionless, frozen and static. According to their view, true object identity is expressed not only by the volume but also by the movement characteristic of real objects. They proclaimed, both in their numerous manifestos and paintings, that static reality is but a fiction, an abstraction from real experience lacking substance and truth. Even if objects surrounding us are not actually moving, they nevertheless appear in motion as the human eye is never at rest. We tend to think that objects are stagnant only because we are ordinarily too busy to pay attention to our inner experience. Nothing we perceive is at rest and moving objects constantly multiply themselves before our eyes. In an actual experience, the dog currently running before my eyes does not have, as we commonly say, only four legs but rather twenty or thirty. Balla's painting, *Dynamism of a Dog on a Leash,* is a clear example of this attempt to represent or reproduce dynamic experiences. Compared with the Cubist ideal, the Futurist goal certainly indicates the rise of a new identity awareness or a richer object identity in the painter's mind who seeks to represent not only the object's volume but also its movement.

Nevertheless, object identity continues to be elusive. What is reality and what is fiction in the things we perceive? Every school of art we mentioned above tended to view its own products as the "true" representation of reality, usually dismissing art products from other schools as "abstractions" lacking substance. But then we have to admit that every painting we discussed above does emphasize an aspect of reality which we all experience. In a sense one would say that they are all "true" or "real," yet all of them together only pronounce the elusiveness of object identity. Where does this identity lie? Is it in the form of the object? The color? The volume or the movement? This elusiveness of object identity becomes even more pronounced when attention is focused on the relations between the object seen and its background. We said earlier that identity is always born in relation to other identities, and the more one studies these relations, the more undefined and vague object identity becomes.

Classic art generally overemphasized the object painted against or at the expense of the background. And there is a message involved in this way of representing objects. The painter tells his audience that whatever is painted in the center of his work is important whereas objects in the background are somewhat like "second class" citizens. A classic painting expresses a value judgment; it takes sides and states what object is more or less important, placing the first in the center and relegating the second to the periphery of the beholder's attention. But then this preferential treatment of central figures or the sacrifice of background objects was considered by Cubist or Futurist painters as a falsification of reality as well as an insult to common sense. In contrast to classic artists, the Futurists insisted that objects are not isolated identities but always appear interrelated with their surrounding environment. Basically this was the contention of Cubism which the Futurists further emphasized. The claim was that the contours of the object seen usually fuse with the environment and the latter penetrates the object and determines its identity. Thus, any artistic product which ignored these dynamic relations between the object and its environment was considered false, unreal, and by some, even "insane."

But when one becomes too sensitive to the relations between object and environment, one soon loses sight of the former. When figures become part of the surrounding milieu and movement becomes a major characteristic of the whole scene, the materiality of bodies is bound to collapse. "To paint a human figure," goes one of the Futurist manifestos, "you must not paint it; rather, you must render the whole of its surrounding atmosphere." Boccioni's painting, *The City Rises,* and Carrà's painting, *Simultaneity—Woman on a Balcony,* exemplify this penetration between the figure and its environment. Severini, another member of the Futurist movement, said: "We wish to enclose the universe in a work of art. Objects no longer exist." The real identity of the object lies, according to this philosophy, in the interplay between its inner life and the dynamism of its environment, or rather in the essential oneness of the two elements. However, this very search for the universal identity of an object in the complexity of its relations to other objects eventually brought about the dissolution of the object in its own environment.

In Balla's painting, *Swifts: Paths of Movement + Dynamic Sequences,* the individual swifts are hardly distinguishable from one another. Their individual forms and the shape of their wings are di-fused by the intensity of their flight. But in this way the wood becomes hidden by the multiplicity of its trees; Balla's painting ceases to be a representation of real objects and instead acquires an abstract quality. Futurism indeed gave expression to a higher level of identity awareness in which the identity of the object appears as a dynamic complex of relations between the individual object and its environment. When the object's relations to other identities in the environment are over-stressed, it gradually becomes fragmented, like the destroyed Tower. We recall that the dispersion of the people of Babel came about through the relation to or conflict with another identity. This holds true, as we shall later see, also for human identity in its relation to the social environment.

We said earlier that two opposing tendencies or features charac-terize man's search for object identity: The classic and the romantic tendencies. Every school of art mentioned above strove to find the "true" and "ultimate" representation of object identity. In so doing, they expressed a classic craving for the most durable form or the most truthful impression of an object. Of course, each school conceived of object identity in its own way. Picasso's classic tendency, for example, differs from Raphael's since the former saw the volume and not the pure form as the basic characteristic of object identity. But in their search for a durable substance of things seen, they both expressed the same classic tendency to look for the essential and most durable aspect of objects. On the other hand, artists, and very often the same artists, were not unaware of the multiplicity of the object's facets, its relations to the possible positions of the beholder as well as its relations to its environment. Opening themselves and yielding to this variety of appearances, artists often lost or cautiously rejected the singularity of one perspective (like the central or frontal) as well as the tendency to focus on one figure. It is in this shift of attention towards the multiplicity of perspectives that romanticism in art begins to announce itself. And we should again emphasize that although we presently limit our discussion of classicism and romanticism to art, we are basically dealing with two cognitive movements of the mind which express themselves in all aspects of human activity. Later chapters will further elaborate this point.

As we have seen earlier, classicism focuses on the center of the field of vision where it tends to erect well organized and architectonic structures of objects. Romanticism, on the other hand, cherishes peripheries of visual fields, twilight zones and hidden corners of nature. In many romantic paintings, the periphery is invested with a higher degree of importance since it is considered fraught with mystery and uncanniness. The half-dark corners of nature, remote and unfrequented niches, are believed to hide deep secrets about life, clues about human fate, etc. And it is therefore implied that the more any object relates to the periphery of its environment, the more it becomes invested with profound meaning and fascination. And we saw that in contrast to the centrality of figure in Raphael's painting, the sharp distinction between center and periphery gradually disappears in the painting of the Cubists and Futurists. The interpenetration of forms and the interdependence of objects that became transparent, allowing the environment to penetrate them, necessarily gave equal weight to both periphery and center in their paintings. This equilibrium between center and periphery, when it indeed exists, is the first expression of the romantic trend of cognition which seeks to relate the object to its environment.

But when this romantic trend is given full expression, the object disappears and dissolves itself in a centrifugal movement which carries it away from the center only to be dispersed in the periphery. Kandinsky's painting *Improvisation* #30 *(Canons)* is one example of a romantic expression. In overstressed romanticism, this de-emphasizing of the center often turns the painting into a formal complex of forms and colors that do not aim to represent any physical object, but rather free the perceiver from all hints of physical reality, sending him back to the free play of his imagination. In fact, many of Kandinsky's paintings constitute a message directed to the beholder, stating that object identity cannot in principle be represented because identity is not an observable phenomenon. According to this philosophy, art ceases to be representational and becomes only *evocative,* corresponding to inner and dynamic experiences where delineated and fixed objects do not exist. Obviously, in extreme expressions of romanticism, reality as well as its artistic expression lose articulation and acquire a dream-like blur or abstraction.

Thus, at both poles of human cognition, the classic and the romantic, identity awareness seems most abstract and the furthest removed from being a fully articulate representation of reality. On the one hand, the focusing on the centrality of the figure and the search for ideal forms of objects distort reality because other, equally important facets of object identity are ignored. The classic figure indeed tends to be an abstract and stagnant representation. On the other hand, romanticism also drives towards abstractions. The lack of focus and the de-emphasizing of the center often turn the painting into an abstract complex of forms and colors that do not even pretend to represent any object and are very often illegible. Therefore, the cognitively "unreal" would reside at both poles of consciousness. A cognition constantly riveted to rigid forms and blind to nature's multiple facets is egocentric, impoverished and unadaptive. On the other hand, adaptability and sanity are not characteristic of minds always in a state of cognitive fluidity or romantic turmoil. We can therefore say that a sane awareness of an object identity lies at a point of balance between the classic and the romantic poles of consciousness. But where is this point of balance in the mind and what is precisely a sane awareness or representation of an object identity? We have to realize that sanity is but a relative determination and the perennial attempt on the part of different schools of art to capture and represent *the* identity of the object seen is but a testimonial to its perpetual elusiveness. We said that identity is born with the use of a concrete sign which is, in this case, imagery. But imagery, not only that of ordinary people but also of creative artists, does not exhaust the scope and richness of object identity. It seems that no image can fully represent it. We look at our faces in the mirror every morning, but do we have a clear image of how we look? Not yet. Yes, we do recognize ourselves and know *in general* how we look. But this awareness always remains incomplete and somewhat murky so that we constantly feel the need to look at our reflections in the mirror or at photographs.

It is amazing, however, how blind we often are to this elusiveness of object identities. Don't we commonly think that objects are something "concrete," "solid," something that always remains the same? Many would say that, after all, everybody knows what the words "dog" and "chair" mean, since they refer to "concrete" objects. But it required the sensitivity of painters and artists to show that objects are not "concrete" in the sense of being complete entities, finished products remaining eternally the same. There are infinite angles from which a chair can be seen and from each angle it looks different. Not only the position of the beholder would determine the way this chair would look but also the intensity of light falling on it, intensity which constantly varies with the position of the sun. No one sees the *same* chair or the *same* table all the time although both might occupy a room which one enters every day. How can people then say that a chair or a table is something "concrete" that always remains the same? It must be the bad influence that words have on the mind. For the word "chair" or "dog" always remains the same, and then people come to believe that what it stands for also remains unchanged. In one of his *Pensées,* Pascal wrote:

> A man is a whole; but suppose we dissect him, what will he be—head, heart, stomach, veins, each vein, blood, all the humors in the blood?
> A city, a plain, seen from a distance, is a city and a plain; but as one draws nearer, there are houses, trees, tiles, leaves, grass, ants, ants' legs, and so on indefinitely. All are included in the word "plain."[6]

It is only from a distance that a city seems small enough to be represented or "summarized," so to speak, by the word "city." The closer we get to the city, the more differentiated our perception becomes and the unity of this city dissolves into the multiplicity of streets, houses, etc. The more extensively we inspect these phenomena, the more we realize how infinite is the number of details that were left out or remained unnoticed by names relating to them. True, words do provide unity; the word "city" does give a unifying outlook to the multiplicity of streets and houses. But it is erroneous to believe that this unity provided by the word "city" is itself the reality it stands for. The reality and identity of a city are as elusive as the reality and identity of a chair or a table.

Since the early days of philosophical thinking, philosophers have been debating whether *universals* exist in reality. Does man *in general,* i.e., not this or that person we see in the street but universal man, exist? Plato indeed believed that beyond this world there is a transcendental reality populated with universal *Ideas* such as universal Good, universal Beauty or universal Man. Following Plato and Aristotle, many philosophers have contended that general concepts such as horse, man, justice, virtue, indeed possess real existence outside the mind. This trend of philosophical thought is known as *realism,* to be contrasted with *nominalism* which contends that only individual entities exist, i.e., only this or that horse, this or that person have reality and that general concepts such as *horse, man,* are only abstractions which the mind draws from individual entities.

But our considerations concerning the elusiveness of all identities indicate that extreme *realism* and extreme *nominalism* are abstractions without basis in reality. Unless we claim to a mystical, unworldly kind of awareness, our ordinary consciousness is aware neither of absolutely universal nor absolutely individual entities. Yes, we do have general notions of what man, city or justice are. But unlike the *words* "justice" and "city" which always remain the same, these notions, as identity awareness, continue to be in the making as they depend on particular instances of cities, men, etc., from which they draw their generality. On the other hand, we never have a complete picture of an individual object as our perception is always constrained by this or that point of view. Our mind rounds off what the eyes see, and what we believe to be an individual person, for example, is already contaminated by general features of man which the mind projects on what is perceived. Thus, in our cognition the general is neither more nor less real than the particular as they are both active components of our perception which always consists of a background and a figure.

Take justice as another example of elusive identity. What do we mean by the word "justice?" The word would refer to modes of action, behaviors that a society would consider acceptable according to its own value system. For instance, hanging a thief or rewarding an act of loyalty might be cases expressing justice. However, lawyers know well how difficult it is to determine in many individual cases where justice ends and injustice begins. Obviously, justice has an identity, for we all refer to something when we pronounce the word. But it is an elusive identity which remains in the making as individual trials establish new precedents and help to redefine the law. Justice is as elusive as any other identity. It is only the word "justice" that remains identical to itself, not what it stands for. In the United Nations, all delegates often use the word "justice," but how often do they all mean the same thing?

Equally elusive are such identities like character or personality. What is personality? Here, too, we encounter the common confusion between words and reality as people tend to believe that words are not mere signifiers but realities. In our mind we often "summarize" most of our acquaintances in labels like "nice," "aggressive," "mean," etc. We tend to consider these words as representing "being" itself, the very existence of the persons concerned whom we "carry," so to speak, in our heads, eternally frozen in these verbal labels. Most of these persons have little chance to change or remove these labels from our minds because we consider the labels to be their real identities.

Not only lay people but also many theoreticians in the field of psychology have been susceptible to this confusion between verbal labels and reality. The debate revolves around the nature of human traits. What is a trait? Broadly defined, a trait is what distinguishes one person from another. For example, the trait of being closefisted would characterize someone who would consistently not give donations to his church as compared to a generous person who would. Now for many psychologists, traits like "closefistedness," "generosity" or "aggressiveness" are not mere words or characterizations referring to certain types of human behavior but rather a psychological reality of some kind, a "mental structure" that really exists within the individual. Thus Freud, Anna Freud, Murray, Allport and others, subscribed to philosophical *realism* in claiming that general traits do have real existence within the person. A series of psychological tests like the Rorschach and the TAT were devised to detect these traits and thereby presumably discover the *real* person.

However, behavioral psychologists like Skinner and Mischel contested the view that general traits have real existence within the person. They have adopted a philosophical *nominalism* in emphasizing that personality should be defined not by general characteristics but rather by the individual acts the person overtly performs. For example, instead of looking for a general trait of aggressiveness supposedly *within* the person under study, they claim that one should study his behavior to detect individual acts of aggression and examine their environmental origin. This approach obviously believes that the environment, both physical and cultural, is the determining factor in the development of all kinds of behavior and that in controlling or changing the environment one can also change man's behavior and, thus his personality. Personality, according to this view, is *nothing more* than the overt acts of the person. The existence of genetic or inner traits is vehemently rejected and Mischel also shows how the huge volume of research studies done with psychological tests generally failed to determine the validity of the existence of those supposedly *real* traits within the person.[7]

We must admit, however, that people often display enough consistency in their behavior to justify ascribing to them labels such as "closefisted" or "generous." It is appropriate to characterize a person who constantly hits other people as an aggressive person. We should remember, however, that traits are nothing but words, labels or signifiers that belong to an observer who wishes to describe or define a certain reality. They are not this reality itself. Interestingly, even the believers in the existence of real traits within the person cannot provide definite, unequivocal descriptions of human identity. The Freudian camp usually describes the person as having dual, opposing traits like "passive-aggressive," "obsessive-compulsive," "dependent-independent," etc. The reality they want to define is too elusive to be exhausted by a single trait. One can adequately label a person "nice", if one notices a certain consistency in his "nice" acts. On the other hand, one should realize that from another point of view and judged according to different criteria, this person may appear "mean." Therefore, this person's identity cannot be reduced either to the "mean" or the "nice" characterizations. It transcends both.

Now, if the identities of the persons we know are elusive, if identities like chairs, faces, figures, justice and virtue are equally difficult to grasp, what is self-identity? Who are we as individuals? Is there a thing called the self? Yes. It is the way one is aware of other identities. Your own way of perceiving the chair, your own views of justice, of virtue or of the world constitute your self-identity. Self-identity is an awareness of the world in one way or another.

My awareness of my world implies certain philosophy, beliefs or value system. I am never aware of the world through "naked eyes." For example, I look at the behavior of others and judge that one behavior is "right" and another is "wrong." This means that I already possess a set of criteria or beliefs with which I perceive and evaluate these behaviors or other identities I encounter. And these beliefs or value system also determine my own behavior. If I adopt certain beliefs as to what constitutes "good," "nice" or "mean" behavior, I will tend to act according to this belief and will therefore develop a trait. I will commit, for example, only "nice" acts and therefore become a "nice" person. My beliefs on matters like morality, charity, love, etc., will determine my behavior and therefore shape my traits which are also the way I am aware of the world and evaluate it. My self-identity is then reflected through my views or outlooks about the world which are also *dispositions* to act in a particular way. For example, my views about women would determine the way I would court them; my basic attitude towards authority would dictate my behavior towards my father or my boss. This could make me a "male chauvinist," a "tender" husband or a "rebellious" man, i.e., could help determine my identity.

Obviously, it is society that provides me with the beliefs and criteria with which I look at and evaluate my world. The eyes with which I examine my world are also public eyes and my self-identity is also a social product. For it is always a specific social culture that tells me what is "good" and "bad," thereby determining my traits or dispositions to act. Society tells me how to be aware of my own world and it therefore determines my identity. However, despite this social influence, my awareness of the world always retains its singularity and uniqueness. For people can teach me how a chair or table looks in general. Still, when I look at the chair, I see it from my particular point of view. I do not see then a chair "in general." By the same token, society develops in me general dispositions to act but when I actually engage myself in a behavior I express these dispositions in my own idiosyncratic ways. For example, people may teach me what "gentlemanly" behavior generally means but I will eventually develop my own individual style of being a gentleman. It will conform to the general norms of "gentlemanliness" but it will also show a particular feature characteristic of me and only me. Certainly I cannot behave like a gentleman "in general." Sometimes I will behave in a certain manner and will be concerned whether my behavior conformed to the general norms of being a gentleman. I will ask other people and they might not have a clear answer. Then I will start to think that one can probably re-define the trait "gentleman" to accommodate my own unorthodox be-havior. Thus, although traits and dispositions are social products, they are constantly influenced, redefined and changed by the idiosyncratic behavior of the individual person.

But this means that my self-identity is not a fixed entity. My awareness of the world and my behavior change as I gradually change my opinions or values. My identity is my awareness of the world but identity awareness swings, as we have said, between the classic and the romantic poles. In a sane mind, all object identities are not static realities but rather a dynamic process of creation. Sanity is not a given fact but a perennial yo-yo game in which identities like a chair, a face, justice or virtue always remain in the making, half-hidden, half-un-veiled, like an image which is constantly being formed, yet never accomplished. This means that self-identity is this oscillation between the classic and the romantic. There is always the classic in you that tells you that you are indeed somebody, i.e., gives you social definitions and labels such as "New Yorker," "Englishman" or "male chauvinist." On the other hand, there is also the romantic in you that constantly makes you feel somewhat vague, undecided or enigmatic, thereby indi-cating that you are an elusive, still unfinished product. And as long as your self-identity or your awareness of the world shuttles between the classic and the romantic modes of cognition, you can consider yourself sane.

CHAPTER 3

Cognitive Towers

What is the nature of the universe? What is reality? Here we will dwell more extensively on ways in which man has depicted the universe for himself. He has developed philosophical ideas, scientific theories and religious beliefs to determine the identity of the universe. But when we study the development of these theories, beliefs and ideas we realize that the identity of the universe has remained as elusive as the identity of the chair or the table we discussed in the previous chapter. We now want to emphasize that what one commonly calls "objective reality" or the universe is not something one finds lying "there" when one is born. Reality or the universe is something one builds together with other people and with the help of beliefs and theories which we call cognitive Towers. Scientific theories or philosophical beliefs are steel girders, so to speak, that man introduces into the world in order to create a meaningful cosmos. But these steel girders or cognitive Towers do not belong to reality itself. They are contributions of the human mind which wants to find meaning in the universe. Man has constantly built cognitive Towers, then abandoned them to build new ones. With this endless activity, the picture of the universe has remained elusive.

Why nights and days, summer and then winter? What is behind this constant change in nature, the fluctuation in temperature, the ebbs and tides, birth and death? There must be a method in the madness, an underlying unity to this dizzying parade of colors, forms or shadows the eyes have to see throughout their existence. And, indeed, man has invented many unifying principles to form and consolidate his universe.

"The central aims of science," Toulmin comments, "are . . . concerned with a search for understanding—a desire to make the cause of nature not just predictable but intelligible—and this has meant looking for rational patterns of connections in terms of which we can make sense of the flux of events.[1]" Creating an "intelligible" world is putting

the events one experiences in a frame of reference, giving them a definition or a *name* such as the one the people of Babel looked for. An
intelligible world is one that has identity, and in search for this identity,
man has employed not only scientific thinking but also mythology,
philosophical beliefs or religious ideas. All these unifying principles
share one common denominator: They are all cognitive beliefs, inventions of the mind. And in forming them, man has expressed his
classic as well as his romantic tendencies. In the previous chapter we
described the formation of identities like a chair or a dog. Here we deal
with larger, more fateful identities like "the universe," "the cosmos" or
"life." But the cognitive process in which these larger identities are
formed is the same. Like any identity, those like "the universe," "life,"
or "God" have always remained elusive, half-unveiled, half-hidden, at
times unified and coherent, at other times vague and diverse. Man has
created his cognitive beliefs after his own image; they both appear as
being constantly in the making.

Somewhere in heaven or beyond the horizon there exists another
world which contrasts with this world; it is real and eternal, not fleeting
and perishable. This has been the most prevailing idea in man's mind
since the beginning of history. And this has also been his way of introducing unity in his existence. The creatures you now see—various,
mutable, ever shifting, ambiguous—are only replicas of heavenly "ori-
ginals" which are *the* real entities in existence. Archaic man always
believed that whatever he encountered or built was rooted and sup-
ported by celestial archetypes. The different horses or cows he saw
found unity in the perfect, truly real horses or cows in the other world.
All objects were considered real only to the extent that they partici-
pated, in one way or another, in a reality that transcended them.[2]

An inhabited city or certain rivers were but copies of celestial
archetypes of cities and rivers. Also, the actions of archaic man were
considered repetitions of "original" gestures first made by other beings
who were not men but gods or semi-gods. Therefore, whenever archaic
man acted, he felt he was repeating the act of creation; every creative
act was but a repetition of the first creative act that brought the entire
cosmos into being. Eating and nutrition in general were not considered
simple physiological acts; they renewed a communion. Marriage and
collective orgies echoed mythical prototypes. They were but repetitions
of what gods, ancestors or old heroes once performed.

This is then how archaic man expressed the classic tendency of his mind. This world receives unity, form or structure from above. It is as if there were reins descending from heaven to hold the maddening variety of earthly phenomena together. We saw earlier that the classic tendency in the mind is highly focused, usually emphasizing the center of any space as the place where most important entities should reside. Archaic thinking displays the same penchant for the center. There was a marked tendency on the part of archaic man to believe that his city, country or temple was indeed situated in the center of the world.[3] Since he considered his house and city copies of celestial models, they naturally had to display the directions of cosmic space. Thus, just as the universe was believed to stretch out towards the four cardinal points, an archaic village was generally built around a center and was divided into four sections corresponding to the division of the universe into four horizons.

And the center of the city was commonly considered a sacred place where a shrine or a temple was built to connect heaven and earth. Also pillars, ladders (Jacob's ladder, for example), sacred mountains and trees were often believed to be the center of the world, the *axis mundi* that connected heaven and earth. Jerusalem and the Temple most commonly fulfilled this role of the center. Thus, the myth of the Tower of Babel only reiterates the emphasis that archaic man laid on the center or on the navel of the earth where heaven and earth meet and communicate with one another.

However, this way of visualizing the world is characteristic not only of archaic thinking but of the human mind in general, independent of any period of history. The Greeks, the initiators of philosophical thinking, also constructed the image of the universe with the help of cognitive Towers. They, too, emphasized a *real* world in contrast to the visible and mutable universe we all perceive, the former generally providing unity to the latter. Thales, for example, who was one of the earliest philosophers in ancient Greece, believed that water is the basic and most real substance in the universe. The identity of every worldly phenomenon is basically water. Anaximenes was more in favor of air as the fundamental substance. He said that God is air and all human souls are air as well. Heracleitos, however, put his trust in fire as the unifying principle of the universe. Imaginary as these theories may now seem, they did not lack rational sophistication. They were the first examples of the reductionist approach which is characteristic of scientific thinking. A modern scientist would speak of magnetic fields or energies as *the* essence of matter. Obviously, modern science employs different methodology, research procedures and measurements than early Greek science. But they both share the basic reductionist approach which seeks to reduce the variety of visible phenomena to one unifying element, be it air, water or magnetic fields.

And most interesting is the recurrent image of the Tower that philosophers have used in describing the unity of the universe. Once the first principle of reality, the unifying *being,* was presumably identified, the whole universe was seen, in a typically classic view, as a pyramid where creatures and objects are hierarchically ranked according to their level of development and importance. From the time of Plato to the present, philosophical thinking has often been dominated by images like Towers, pyramids or chains as being the underpinnings of the universe.

In his book *The Great Chain of Being,* Lovejoy describes this sway that Plato's philosophy has had over Western thinking. He shows how Plato introduced the idea of a cosmic hierarchy of all beings, all tied together by a great chain which:

> . . . Is composed of an immense or . . . an infinite number of links ranging in hierarchical order from the meagerest kind of existents, which barely escapes nonexistence, through 'every possible' grade up to the *ens perfectissimum* . . . every one of them differing from that immediately above and that immediately below by the 'least possible' degree of difference.[4]

At the top of the pyramid lies, as Plato describes in his *Timaeus,* the Supreme Being, or the *Idea* of the *Good.* This supreme being is the most perfect and most real of all realities, the creator of the universe and its ultimate principle. And because it is perfect, it is filled with goodness and bounty, and the world was created by "emanation." God or the Supreme Being would not be absolutely good had he jealously deprived reality, or life, of worldly entities. The universe was created by the emanation of his goodness that "overflowed," so to speak, and brought all entities into being.

In this sense, no worldly creature or object is isolated or lonely. They all belong to one unity. At the bottom of the pyramid you will find the most imperfect creatures on earth ranked according to a continuum that gradually rises towards its origin and ultimate unity, the Supreme Being. Very often philosophers, especially in the era of the Enlightenment, stressed this continuity among worldly entities. First inanimate matter, then primitive vegetation, then earthworms, then animals, man and God. They all form one family. We saw earlier that identity awareness of an object obtains when its various aspects are simultaneously grasped or perceived in a coordinated fashion. Similarly, philosophical theories commonly established the identity of the universe by demonstrating, as far as they could, that indeed *all* worldly entities reflect the first principle of reality: All creatures show the glory of the Creator.

Throughout the years, Plato's ideas were recast in different forms and Lovejoy's book carefully records the successive expressions it received in various times. Different philosophers conceived of the first principle of reality in different ways. Once Christianity entered the scene, Plato's ideas were recast in theological terms and the Supreme Being became the Judaeo-Christian God. On the other hand, in the age of the Enlightenment with its deistic trends, reason assumed the role of the first principle of reality, systematically tying worldly phenomena hierarchically with the help of natural laws. In this sense, God was believed to have revealed Himself in the universal law of nature which the scientist was eager to discover and study.

It is obvious that towers, mythical mountains linking earth and heaven, pyramids or hierarchical chains are all vertical constructions. Both mythological imagery and philosophical thinking often portrayed the universe as a huge vertical edifice rising upward towards the skies where its ultimate origin lies. But other spatial directions such as the circular or the horizontal were also used in the cognitive construction of the universe, not necessarily replacing the vertical direction but complementing it. Thus, while the universe maintains its vertical thrust, life within the universe may appear as a cyclical movement. Many archaic as well as Greek beliefs stressed the cyclical course of creation in which life alternates with death, souls transmigrate and all entities appear and disappear in the "eternal repetition of the same," to use Nietzsche's expression. On the other hand, the Judaeo-Christian tradition has stressed the horizontal rather than the cyclical direction. The world was created at a certain point in the past and is now progressing like a river towards a certain point in the future. Here one may speak of a horizontal Tower providing unity and meaning to the variety of events and entities in this world. According to this religious tradition, every event receives its meanings from the ultimate goal in the future, every happening is only one step further towards the Day of Judgment or Salvation. Each occurrence is but another evidence of the master plan in nature which orients all beings towards this crucial day.

In the era of the Enlightenment, this Judaeo-Christian conception was given a secular form. Such is the idea of *progress* in history.[5] Filled with an optimism rooted in the new commercial and industrial development, many thinkers felt that history was constantly progressing toward eventual prosperity, the triumph of reason and the establishment of eternal peace. This was the age of Godwin, Condorcet, Smith and Kant, who echoed much of the new enthusiasm accompanying economic expansion and scientific development. However, when flaws in the economic system of the age became conspicuous, when poverty and misery struck thousands in industrial cities, the faith in the bourgeois idea of progress started to fade. This, however, did not necessarily change the faith of people in the continuous and forward movement in history. It was only the ultimate goal that was altered. Marx and Engels conceived a new secular guise for the old Judaeo-Christian messianic vision. They preached that world history was basically the history of struggles between social classes, necessarily leading to the socialist salvation i.e., the revolution of the proletariat.

It really does not matter in which direction man has erected his cognitive Towers. Whether the steel girders he casts are vertical or horizontal, in each case they express the classic tendency of his mind to organize the world into a single unity. And, undoubtedly, each time man created a cosmos he felt secure, confident and even superior. Archaic man put himself in the middle of the world, constantly in touch with heavens and gods through his temples, towers or sacred mountains that scraped the skies. It was a vision that instilled a sense of security and belonging. The cosmos was believed to have come into existence from its center; it marked the way every embryo develops.[6] Rising high from the center of the earth towards the sky, a sacred mountain or a temple filled archaic man with pride, power and the sense of identity; and not less powerful and impressive was the universe of the Greeks or the one envisioned by rationalistic philosophers such as Spinoza or Leibnitz. The latter was convinced that this world, as he saw it, was the best of all possible worlds. The classic vision has the tendency to look for and believe in perfect forms.

We said earlier that identity is established in relation or in opposition to other identities that keep impinging on its boundaries, frequently threatening to encroach. In archaic thinking, the center of the earth—the main source of identity or security—is adjacent to a dark region where chaos reigns supreme.[7] In many cases, the center of the earth, the gate to heaven and the entry to this dark region were believed to be situated on the same axis along which the passage from one cosmic region to another was effected. In other words, the center of the world was constantly threatened by dark forces that aimed to destroy the organized world, reinstating formlessness or chaos.

According to Eliade,[8] it is highly probable that the fortifications of inhabited places and cities both in Europe and in other continents began by being magical defenses. Trenches, ramparts, labyrinths, etc., were designed to repel invasion by demons and souls rather than attacks by human beings. During the Middle Ages in Europe, inherited habits from archaic ages were still maintained. For example, the walls of cities were ritually consecrated as a defense against the devil, sickness and death. The world of archaic man was therefore penetrable and fragile and the security it offered was constantly threatened by the forces of hell and the ambiguity of the unknown.

Furthermore, despite his central view of the cosmos and his craving for unity, the mythologically oriented mind also believed in the existence of a multiplicity of gods that ruled and influenced the universe while constantly fighting among themselves as well as with man. Thus, the classically clear vision of a cosmic order which brought identity and meaning to the universe was counterbalanced by a romantic vision of a universe tragically, joyously or comically fragmented by strife, torn apart by the impulsive wishes of whimsical gods. To the archaic mind, the world was both clear and murky, well shaped and fragmented, known and unknown.

Philosophical and scientific thinking also show this constant swing between the classic and romantic poles of cognition. The pre-Socratic philosophers were constantly preoccupied by the contrast between the One and Many, the unity and plurality in the universe. And since the days of Parmenides who stressed the unity of "Being" and Heracleitos who emphasized the variegation of "Becoming," philosophers and scientists have been trying in one way or another to demonstrate the unity of the universe within the diversity of phenomena it always displays. Plato bequeathed to philosophers and scientists the idea of a cosmic hierarchy, a metaphysical Tower that provides such a unity. The question is whether this Tower or any Tower, could indeed hold together the multiplicity of worldly phenomena for a long time. The answer is in the negative, as it appears that adverse circumstances as well as the romantic part of the human mind tend to sap the foundations of all Towers.

Having described the various forms in which Plato's cosmic hierarchy appeared in the history of philosophy, Lovejoy points to the 19th century as the age in which the Great Chain of Being was first shaken and destroyed by the romantic movement.[9] In the 18th century the idea of a cosmic hierarchy attained its widest diffusion as many philosophers considered the world a perfectly rational structure. But as the 18th century came to a close, the romantic spirit then sweeping Europe depicted a different view of the universe. In contrast to the rationalist philosophers who stressed unity and order in nature, romantic thinkers like Novalis, Schlegel and Kierkegaard emphasized the unique, incompatible, diversified and mysterious in nature. Lovejoy considers the romantic movement of the 19th century a major historical revolution that terminated the impressively long period during which Plato's ideas concerning hierarchy and order in the universe were prevalent. From that point onward, the world's image began to seem fragmented and "irrational." The focal vision of the classic mind gave place to the unbridled, erratic vision of the romantic spirit.

But Lovejoy is wrong in two points. He believes that the idea of cosmic hierarchy first appeared in Plato's philosophy. We saw, on the other hand, that visions of cosmic Towers, *axis mundi* or ladders that connect heaven and earth pervaded the mythical imagery of archaic man. Plato only gave these visions a philosophical, more "rational" attire. Secondly, Lovejoy believes that the concept of universal hierarchy and cosmic unity was first abolished by the romantic movement of the 19th century. This is also mistaken since romantic revolutions occurred time and again during history, constantly alternating with periods during which "rationality" reigned. While discussing the history of scientific development, Toulmin mentions the ". . . Romantic Syndrome that has recurred every 120 or 130 years for centuries— along with artistic mannerism, drugs and long hair."[10]

It would be helpful to compare in this context two studies, the one is Kuhn's *The Structure of Scientific Revolutions*[11] and the other is O'Dea's *The Sociology of Religion*.[12] There is a striking similarity between the ways both science and religion take form as cultural events in the history of societies. In many cases, it is even difficult to separate the two as they are both cognitive systems designed to give form and structure to the universe. Scientific rigor often appears together with religious ideas. To take one example, Newton did not consider gravity a theoretical construct (as a modern scientist would) or a material force. He rather believed that gravity is a spiritual force indicating God's presence and continuous action in the world.[13] The comparision of Kuhn's and O'Dea's studies will show how the classic and romantic tendencies of the human mind have continuously interacted in the formation of scientific as well as religious beliefs.

A key concept in Kuhn's analysis of the history of scientific development is the concept of *paradigm*. It is an encompassing concept which stands for the entire constellation of scientific beliefs as well as techniques that a scientific community possesses at a certain period. A paradigm tells the scientist what the universe contains and what it does not contain, and what instruments or methodology should be applied in scientific research. But most important, a paradigm determines the identity not only of the universe but also of the scientist. For a paradigm provides specific labels, names and language that determine what is scientifically relevant or irrelevant. To illustrate, a materialist philosopher would believe that the universe is composed of microscopic corpuscles or of other material elements and would therefore tend to explain every phenomenon materialistically, rejecting mentalistic concepts like "soul" or "mind" as mere abstractions or even nonsense. Thus the accepted paradigm would determine what is scientifically "acceptable" or "irrelevant" and the scientific community believing in it would admit to its ranks no member who uses different scientific concepts or language.

A paradigm, then, is a philosophical Tower. It not only serves as an outlook on the universe but it also prescribes the action, language and methods of communication for the members of the scientific community that adopts it. In this sense it gives identity to the scientist as well as to the universe. And once it is accepted, scientists start to extend its scope, applying it to yet unresolved problems. Kuhn calls the ordinary, day to day research activity of the scientist a "puzzle-solving activity." The scientist constantly attempts to explain new phenomena by reducing them to the accepted paradigm.

But paradigms tend to collapse by way of revolutions and what starts this process is first the increasing awareness of *anomaly*. Scientists come to see that nature somehow violates their expectations and the accepted paradigm has ceased to "fit" nature. This is similar to the awareness acquired in art that a classic painting, despite its focused nature and classical clarity, represents only a few aspects of the object, neglecting its many other facets. Following this awareness of anomaly or gaps between scientific theory and reality, there begins a period of pronounced professional insecurity or a crisis in which a multiplicity of natural phenomena appear unexplained and discrepant with the accepted paradigm. And in response to this crisis a new paradigm is born in a flash of insight or intuition that brings about a scientific revolution.

Kuhn compares scientific revolutions with political revolutions that aim to change established institutions which have become incapable of responding to the needs of society. In each case revolutions are preceded by a state of crisis calling for a new paradigm, new steel girders to construct the universe, explain away discrepancies and provide a new meaning to existence. But similar to the plurality of political factions, each claiming to have the right political answer for a social crisis, different scientific paradigms usually compete for scientific supremacy, each claiming to be the solution for the scientific crisis. Eventually, one paradigm gains the upper hand, not necessarily —as Kuhn emphasizes[14]—through logic and experiments alone but also through techniques of public persuasion. It is important to note however, that the new paradigm brought by a scientific revolution is a totally new creation, a new outlook of the universe and not a mere addition to or modification of an old paradigm. It is a new image or identity given to the world, excluding other possible identities. It therefore defines new concepts and rejects old ones, and its defenders often have to battle for it with the zeal of revolutionaries. But the supremacy of a paradigm tends to be limited as the paradigm soon appears incapable of explaining increasing number of phenomena. At this point a scientific crisis develops and the image of the universe loses its unified nature, and once more the revolutionary process is under way to give birth to a new paradigm.

Not different in structure is the development of religious beliefs. What Kuhn calls *crisis*, O'Dea refers to as a *breaking point* although the latter term conveys an emotionally deeper meaning. But both terms basically refer to a cognitive crisis. There comes a moment when man's existing beliefs no longer help him to explain and cope with his world, and he is then filled with apprehensions and anxieties. O'Dea emphasized three characteristics of the human condition, three factors in life that are likely to bring man to the breaking point: contingency, powerlessness and scarcity. There is always an unpredictable or contingent element in existence which inevitably baffles man's best calculated plans. And in the face of the unexpected, whether it is illness or death, he realizes his basic powerlessness as well as the scarcity of resources that would help him grapple with his predicaments. Breaking points come in moments of extreme despair when man's usual means of coping appear of no avail. He might then undergo a religious conversion and turn to supernatural powers for assistance and comfort.

Religious movements start, as shown by Weber[15] and O'Dea,[16] with the religious *charisma*. It is a subjective experience in which man establishes the first contact with a transcendent world and thereby finds not only new ways of handling his predicaments but an altogether new meaning for his existence. *Charisma* is a creative act that establishes a new identity as well as unity for the group of believers: It gives them a *name* in the same sense that the people of Babel clung to a *name*. But charismatic phenomena are tentative, fleeting and rare. Many generations might witness only one prophet, if any at all. Therefore, in order to prolong its existence and remain influential, *charisma* must find a palpable or concrete dimension, a Tower, that would guarantee its historical continuity. Identity requires, as we said earlier, a tangible sign. Usually *charisma* transforms itself into a structured and hierarchical "establishment" of clergy, thereby becoming institutionalized. Institutionalization also entails the formulation of worship patterns or cults which specify numerous ways that accentuate the believer's belonging to a specific religious sect. Definite words, prayers, symbols and rituals become signs of religious identity through which the believer can relive the original charismatic experience. Prayers and rituals add objective and concrete dimensions to the originally subjective and fleeting experience of *charisma,* thereby securing its continuity throughout time.

Perhaps the best example of religious institutionalization literally resembling a tower is the Catholic Church. According to the Catholic faith, the original *charisma* is historically preserved and transmitted from one generation to another by the Apostolic Succession. This is an unbroken line of succession connecting the first Apostles to the existing hierarchy of bishops and priests, and the salvation of the believer is conditional upon his acceptance of this hierarchy and belonging to the Christian community. In other words, the Church has become the objective and concrete representation of the originally spontaneous and subjective experience of the religious *charisma*.

The "Thou shalts" and "Thou shalt nots," the various rituals and the clerical hierarchy, all these concrete dimensions of religion express, above all, man's classic tendency or his aspiration for a harmonious and orderly image of the universe as well as identity and definition for himself. It is the same classical tendency which expresses itself in art, mythology and philosophical theories. The emblems and rituals of religion infuse the believer with a sense of identity, belonging and security because they define the world in a way as to make it compatible to him. It is through them that a functional goal of religion is fulfilled: Within the religious "establishment" man is reconciled with his world, his anxieties are alleviated and the gap separating him from the transcendent Being is bridged. Even critics like Feuerbach, Marx and Freud, who rejected religion on the basis of its "irrationality," fully confirmed this funtional role of religion for the believer.

But religion is not only functional; it is also dysfunctional. It expresses not only man's classical aspirations but also his romantic tendencies. Religion brings to man not only harmony and concord but also dissonance and discord. First to be noticed is that in the very beginning of their existence, religious movements inevitably lead to clashes with the existing orders of society, both secular and religious.[17] Also, religious identity, like any identity, is born and maintained at the expense of, or in constant relation to, other identities. By acquiring a new self-definition or a new identity, a religious movement also defines what it *is not,* i.e., distinguishes itself from or rejects another identity. This rejection of other identities is as essential to religious movements as are their positively defined values. Indeed, the three monotheistic religions have never ceased to relate either defensively or offensively to one another. Also, they have never been completely freed from the old Manichean opposition between good and evil, light and darkness. The contrast between God and the Devil, Christ and Anti-Christ, has often been turned into witch-hunts within society or open wars between societies. The words "devil" and "enemy" are frequently synonyms.

That religion arouses feelings of contrast or disharmony as well as evoking beatific imagery and a sense of reconciliation is demontrated in the religious rituals themselves.[18] Being an objectification or institutionalization of the original charismatic experience, cults and rituals on the one hand reënact the worshipper's ties with the original charismatic moment and reaffirm his belonging to a specific religious community. This is the classical aspect of religion which finds its expression in the functional role of rituals. On the other hand, cult and rituals also arouse anxieties and trigger disharmony or "romantic unrest" within the believer.

Rituals usually relate to or consecrate marginal situations, crises or fateful decisions. Prayers accompany birth, death, illness, marriage, etc. It is obvious that in the occurrence of these events, life's precariousness and man's natural vulnerability become most pronounced. Child delivery, for example, although primarily a happy occasion, also arouses a high level of apprehension because of the hazards involved in the delivery itself, birth defects, medical complications, etc. Therefore, rituals or prayers relating to childbirth, marriage or any other important event are not only reassuring but also somewhat overwhelming or awe inspiring. In his prayers or rituals or thanksgiving for attaining a desired goal or escaping an almost certain death, the worshipper, besides being consoled and reassured, also relives part of the anxieties and fear associated with fateful events. Rituals do not evoke only positive experience by allaying anxieties and dissipating doubts; they also arouse anxieties, and apprehensions, as well as mystify the believer's soul. The religious experience of blissful harmony or beatitude is potentiated by contrasting feelings of romantic mystery, apprehension or anxiety. Thus, it is erroneous to assume that the attainment of beatitude through the experience of a classically harmonious picture of the world as it is depicted by many religious writings is the only goal of religions. Many writers, including Bergson[19] and Kierkegaard,[20] specifically accentuated the romantic aspect of religion which assumingly frees man from the bounds of finality, driving him beyond the narrow limits, labels and definitions of this world towards an unknown, more meaningful existence.

Defining itself in opposition to other identities (either secular or religious), religion thereby carries in itself the possibility of conflicts and wars which might bring down its institutions from the outside. But like scientific paradigms or philosophical Towers, religion often disintegrates because of a "mismatch" between its content and human reality; it becomes obsolete and incapable of meeting the spiritual needs of people. The institutionalization of a religious *charisma,* while being a necessary step guaranteeing its historical continuity, also makes it lose its energy, vitality and spontaneity. Routinized observance of religious rituals most often empties them of their meaning and they lose the flexibility needed to satisfy the believer's emotional needs. Sooner or later, reality again brings man to a "breaking point" which, like the "crisis" in the history of scientific development, makes the established religious institution tumble. At that time, man again finds himself overwhelmed by the ambiguities and confusion of his condition awaiting a new revelation or a new *charisma.*

But religious institutions or Towers fall not only because of the objective vicissitudes of life that make them obsolete or because of external attack on their citadels. We saw that the unity of the people of Babel dissolved not only because of God's punishment imposed from the outside but also because of the people's own resistance to this unity. Similarly, it is also man's subjective attitude towards religion that accounts for the dissolution of its institutions. Man's reflective thinking often gives rise to *doubts* that impinge upon and corrode the citadels of any religious institution from within. In O'Dea's words, "Religion, once established does not provide secure and permanent answers. Life and thought continue to drive man beyond the established institutionalized answers and their representation in religious forms. *Doubt* comes into existence as a fundamental breaking point within the religious context."[21] By the same token, the scientist's endless "puzzle-solving activity" as described by Kuhn, although trying only to extend the application of an existing scientific paradigm to yet unresolved problems, usually leads to the discovery of discrepancies and anomalies, eventually contributing to the collapse of the paradigm. Although eager to solve a puzzle, alleviate fears or find identity, man also actively looks for a new puzzle or new anxieties that make him resist fixed identities. Although fearing existential crises, he somehow manages to provoke them. This is the romantic part of his nature.

Like the people of Babel who were reluctant to choose a specific name and assume a fixed identity, man has never attributed to the Supreme Being or God a clearly defined and fixed identity. Part of God has always remained hidden and mysterious. Throughout the history of philosophy, God's attributes were usually expressed negatively, as being different from those known to man. The elusive God

ILLUSTRATIONS

Raphael: *Madonna of the Goldfinch*. About 1505-6.
Oil on panel, 42$\frac{1}{8}$" x 30$\frac{1}{4}$".
Scala, New York/Uffizi, Florence.

Claude Monet: *The Houses of Parliament, Sunset.* 1903.
Oil on canvas, 32" x 36⅜".
National Gallery of Art, Washington.
Chester Dale Collection.

Pablo Picasso: *Les Demoiselles d'Avignon.* 1907.
Oil on canvas, 8' x 7' 8".
Collection, The Museum of Modern Art, New York.
Acquired through the Lillie P. Bliss Bequest.

Pablo Picasso: *Daniel-Henry Kahnweiler*. 1910.
Oil on canvas, 39⅝″ x 28⅝″.
Courtesy of The Art Institute of Chicago.

Giacomo Balla: *Dynamism of a Dog on a Leash.* 1912.
Oil on canvas, 35¾″ x 43⅜″.
Albright—Knox Art Gallery, Buffalo, New York.
Courtesy George F. Goodyear and The Buffalo Fine Arts Academy.

Umberto Boccioni: *The City Rises*. 1910.
Oil on canvas, 6' 6½" x 9' 10½".
Collection, The Museum of Modern Art, New York.
Mrs. Simon Guggenheim Fund.

Carlo Carrà: *Simultaneity—Woman on a Balcony.* 1913.
Oil on canvas, 57⅜" x 52⅜".
Collection, Dr. Riccardo Jucker, Milan.

Giacomo Balla: *Swifts: Paths of Movements + Dynamic Sequences.* 1913.
Oil on canvas, 38⅛" x 47¼".
Collection, The Museum of Modern Art, New York.
Purchase.

Wassily Kandinsky: *Improvisation No. 30.* 1913.
Oil on canvas, 43⅝″ x 43⅝″.
Courtesy of The Art Institute of Chicago.

Leonardo da Vinci: *Mona Lisa*. About 1505.
Oil on panel, 30¼″ x 20⅞″.
Scala, New York/Louvre, Paris.

or *deus absconditus* has been referred to as *not* like this or *not* like that, adding only that it is something far better.[22] For example, God is not powerful or wise in the human sense of power and wisdom, but something far wiser or more powerful. Attributes like "omnipotent" or "most perfect," although giving the impression of being positive predicates of God, at best convey only a negative meaning, i.e., God is not perfect or potent in the human sense of the terms. After all, no one really understands what "omnipotence" or "perfection" actually means. Thus, God has never received a name. When asked for his name, God answered Moses: "I will be what I will be." Later he also told Moses: "But you cannot see my face; for man shall not see me and live." One would lose interest in God, man and the universe once their identities were grasped clearly or summarized by definite names and labels. God's identity, as well as the identity of the universe, always remain in the making, half-hidden, half-revealed, constantly beyond the reach of sky-scraping Towers. Doubt, whether in religion or science, is the vehicle by which man discards fixed identities and resumes his search for God, for the universe or for his own self.

We said that self-identity is basically awareness of the world or of objects within the world. Therefore, to the extent that man crystallizes the image he has of his world he also acquires self-identity. When he constructs his cognitive Towers, he thereby determines his own life style, actions, hopes, dreams, in brief, his own identity. A religious belief would shape his conduct, a philosophical conviction about the universe would determine the decisions he makes. Socrates believed in the world of Ideas, presumably the most perfect and real existence beyond the visible universe. And this belief determined his life as well as his decision to die. He was happy to drink the hemlock and expire, being convinced that death is the release of the soul from the shackles of the body and its return to the eternal existence of the world of Ideas. Within the global philosophical Tower he constructed, Socrates also established the role he had to play in life.

Not only the people he belongs to or the language he speaks determines the identity of a person. Equally important for self-definition is the role one plays in life. There is no person "in general" or an "individual" in the abstract. These words remain empty unless one qualifies them with role descriptions. In reality, people appear as roles and not simply as "persons." There is the role of the father, the role of the wife or the role of the son. There are the roles of a physician, an undertaker, a blue collar worker or a priest. Each role is a cognitive Tower structuring the entire existence of a person and determining his behavior. A person goes to school, studies for years, then works hard to examine the bodies of people, counting their pulses, prescribing medicines and, finally, billing them. Why does he do all that? To fulfil his role as a physician and maintain his self-identity. And roles prescribe what a person can or cannot do. To be a man or a woman is not simply a biological fact, but a social role one has to fulfil.

It is society that determines what the roles are and which role is available to a particular person. Not every citizen (in itself a role) can become a king and some societies do not have the role of a king at all. It is the social milieu that dictates how to be a woman or how to be a wife, a man or a husband. And this obviously differs from one society to another. Arab women and men and American women and men are not the same, as each society prescribes a different role for them. But this difference originates in the belief system or the cognitive Tower each society adopts. Religious or scientific beliefs not only portray images of the universe but also determine the roles of the individuals living in it. A witch doctor in a primitive society and a physician in a modern one fulfil their roles in different ways as the two societies entertain different beliefs about the universe.

However, roles do not create absolute uniformity among people. A culture might define the roles of a woman and a man but then each woman or each man would play the role in a personal way. No two persons fulfil the role of a priest or a cobbler alike. You may know in general what is womanhood or priesthood but when you try to define precisely what women and priests are as individuals you are at a loss. Furthermore, the personal way in which individual people fulfil their roles eventually leads to a redefinition of the role itself. For example, the contemporary role of being a woman is being continuously redefined as women question and alter the traditional definitions of this role.

Thus, cognitive Towers determine the identity of the universe, of God or of the person. Nevertheless, these identities have always retained their elusiveness. Many people commonly imagine the universe as a colossal, solid rock which has always been "there," independent of man's existence and thought. Indeed, as crude matter that impinges on man's senses, this world has always been "there." But as a meaningful whole, as a cosmos contrasting with chaos, this world does depend on man's consciousness and cognitive Towers which introduce meaning into existence. As a meaningful cosmos, the world is then much more malleable than one would think. It can be refurbished, remodeled or completely changed as man continues to create his cognitive Towers.

Even the past can be changed although many would say that it cannot be undone, that it resembles a mountain one cannot move, bypass or get rid of. One hears people complain about how their past haunts them all the time, making them feel embarrassed or guilty. Nevertheless, the past is more manipulable than it seems. Surely we cannot change the traces of the past or the events that took place. But we can change their *meaning* and it is in this sense that the past is changeable.

Take for example the figure of Napoleon. No one can change the events he helped create nor can we alter their sequence. However, their meaning is not a foregone conclusion. Right now, in different parts of the world there are surely many students preparing theses on Napoleon, or on France under his rule. If one takes the time to read these studies, each will present Napoleon in a different light. It is like a kaleidoscope; Napoleon's image keeps changing as studies give different meanings to his actions and to all the events that took place at that time. By the same token, no person can change the events that took place in his life. But these events and all traces of the past resemble the pieces of evidence the jury has to put together in order to determine the reality of the crime. It is only when they say "guilty" that this reality is established, and even then it might be subject to an appeal. Therefore, one can look back at his past, examine it with different criteria and thereby change its meaning or the verdict of "guilty" or "innocent" he had previously passed on himself.

Thus, the world as a meaningful whole, a cosmos both in the physical and the cultural sense, is not something man "finds" but rather something one builds. But the picture of this cosmos constantly crystallizes and dissolves as man provides different meanings to what he sees. Earlier we talked about the existential yo-yo game characterizing the process of formation of all identities. Here it would be appropriate to outline the image that Plotinus depicted of the world. This philosopher lived in the third century A.D. and he was keenly aware of the yo-yo movement characterizing the development of all identities.

Imagine the cosmos as an immense ball without boundaries, or as an unlimited entity extending to all directions. In semi-poetical, semi-philosophical language, Plotinus called the first principle of reality the *One*.[23] The *One* is an infinite creative power, an unlimited energy which gives birth to the finite things which you see around you. The absolute unity of the *One* differentiates itself into the multiplicity of finite creatures in a downward movement. First created is the Mind with its various logical functioning; next comes the plurality of Souls followed by the multiplicity of material objects. The world is therefore created in a Fall or a downward movement and man is believed to belong partly to the realm of spirit or souls, partly to the realm of evil matter. Man can therefore look either upward towards the *One* or downward towards matter, thereby determining his destiny.

According to Plotinus, what is essential to this process of creation is the continuous aspirations of all creatures to contemplate their ultimate unity, the return to the *One*. In differentiating itself into a multiplicity of beings, reality is filled with guilt and remorse. The birth of finite entities is a defection or a sinful separation from the original unity of the *One*. It is like the guilt one experiences when, building his own individual life, he forsakes his family, mother country or original culture. On the one hand, differentiation is an expression of creativity, spontaneity and growth. On the other hand, it is a revolt against original unity or identity, accompanied by remorse and guilt. Thus, like the yo-yo game, the differentiation of the *One* into a multiplicity of creatures is at the same time a contemplation of and a constant drive towards the original unity.

We recall the symbolism of the story concerning the people of Babel, the sexual connotation of the erected Tower, the differentiation of this unity into new nations and new languages. It is the same yo-yo movement that Plotinus wants to describe in his own poetic language. And it is again the yo-yo movement that looms through historical descriptions (like Kuhn's and O'Dea's books) of how man forms his universe with the help of cognitive Towers, how this universe disintegrates, so to speak, when man's theories fail to accommodate its various phenomena and how the universe is recrystallized with the birth of new theories, whether religious, scientific or mythological in nature. The formation of the identity of the universe resembles the cognitive development of any identity formation. It is a constant swing between unity and diversity, between the classic and romantic poles of consciousness.

We can now ask: what is there in man's nature or biological make up that would explain his craving for Towers or this constant swing between the classic and the romantic frames of mind? When psychologists tried to find the cause for man's behavior, they most commonly stressed the organism's biological needs and their demands for gratification. Thus, like a squirrel scurrying around to ferret out seeds and satisfy its hunger, we all engage in behaviors geared to gratify our needs to eat, drink, multiply and survive. In academic language, this explanation of behavior is known as the *homeostatic* principle which states that all organisms seek to maintain a biological *status quo.* Biological urges like hunger or thirst upset this balance, creating an unpleasant tension which continues to irritate the body until it is discharged through the gratification of these urges. In this sense, man's persistent attempts to build Towers could be explained by his needs to gratify his biological urges, build a haven for himself and survive.

Indeed many thinkers have traditionally seen this state of quiescence within the organism as the ultimate goal of any behavior or of life in general. Freud associated pain with an increase of biological tension and pleasure with its discharge, believing that all behavior seeks to attain maximum pleasure in the total absence of tension. In *Beyond The Pleasure Principle*,[24] he even postulated the existence of a death wish in man which constantly pushes him towards aggression and self-destruction because in death he can ultimately achieve complete freedom from all unconscious tensions. In one way or another, the elimination of either spiritual or bodily tension has been often considered the ultimate goal of life, and if this goal cannot be achieved on earth, there must be another world where man can find peace and quiescence. One can detect this general view about the goal of life in the notion of *Nirvana,* in the concept of *vita beata* promised to the Christian believer, in Isaiah's vision about the day when "the wolf shall dwell with the lamb, and the leopard shall lie with the kid," as well as in the recurrent promises of politicians concerning an imminent world peace.

However, that all behavior seeks to attain biological quiescence is only half the truth. Scientists have noticed that the organism cannot tolerate a complete absence of stimulation or tension.[25] A certain level of tension, arousal or anxiety is necessary to maintain proper functioning. Boredom or lack of stimulation is so noxious that it is often used to break the spirits of prisoners and make them cooperate with their jailors.

Various experimental studies have shown how the organism actively engages in activities which are not associated with the gratification of biological needs. One study showed how monkeys worked hard and learned to solve complicated problems for a reward which was not food or water but merely the opportunity to look at the activity in the laboratory around their cell.[26] They were therefore motivated simply by the sight of something "interesting," as if they were on a window-shopping trip. In another study, rats chose to go the long way around a maze to get a reward because this gave them a more complex experience, whereas the short cut would have made things "too simple."[27] Other studies in the functioning of the brain discovered areas where stimulation or increase in tension would create a feeling of pleasure. When electrodes were implanted in these areas in the brain, rats deliberately administered shocks to themselves, obviously enjoying the stimulation.[28] Thus, the organism does not only seek gratification of biological needs or discharge of tension but also a moderate increase in tension. The human infant would indeed look for the breast to nurse, but already at the second day of his life he will focus his attention longer on contours and contrasts of colors than on plain surfaces. While nursing he will tend to concentrate on his mother's eyes because of their black-white contrast.[29] The romantic tendency of the human mind in seeking the intriguing, the incongruent or the ambiguous shows itself at a very early age.

It is difficult, however, to determine what causes this or that particular behavior in man or whether he is motivated by the increase or decrease of his inner tension. Brain research shows that pleasure is also derived from a simultaneous decrease and mild increase in biological tension.[30] At first glance it would seem plausible to assume that man's classic tendencies make him build cognitive Towers in order to satisfy his biological needs, and that his romantic drives make him seek excitement by abandoning these Towers and wandering to the periphery of his universe where the unknown and the intriguing reside. But the classic and the romantic tendencies of the mind often express themselves simultaneously. Man indeed seeks to gratify his hunger but the bread he bakes for himself offers, besides, a variety of aesthetic shapes and colors that please the imagination. Clothes do not only protect against the cold but also stimulate the eye. Also, man would like some degree of suspense to accompany his efforts to gratify his needs or else life would be intolerably boring. For example, the mild anxiety accompanying the anticipation of the arrival of a lover only adds to the pleasure experienced upon arrival. The painful memories of separation and loneliness only intensify a renewed relationship or reconciliation. It seems reasonable to assume that in most cases classic and romantic tendencies interact to motivate man's behavior. We saw that, while adopting a religious belief or a scientific theory, man's doubting spirit or "puzzle-solving" curiosity remains active and eventually shakes the foundations of these cognitive Towers. It seems that man wants to be gratified while being at the same time aroused in a different way; he wants to build Towers while thinking of changing or constantly modifying their shape. In other words, he wants to play the yo-yo game of existence.

Play as a human behavior has often been defined in contradistinction to more purposeful, functional activity. Ordinarily, parents would tell their children that there is time to play and time to work, thereby implying that these two activities do not go together. In this sense, work is considered a purposeful or "serious" activity striving to achieve a goal, whereas play is seen as an activity engaged in for its own sake. Also, Piaget distinctly distinguishes play from the functional, adaptive behavior of the mind. Whereas in the normal course of adaptive behavior the mind both assimilates reality to its already established concepts as well as changes these concepts to accommodate reality, in play it only assimilates reality to its whimsical inventions.[31] In other words, in play man hovers, so to speak, over life, neglecting the demands of reality while enjoying the freedom of his imagination which creates "as ifs," imaginary constructions of reality. Summarizing the various theories and studies, Ellis ties play in with the organism's need to seek stimulation or tension increase, whereas functional behavior or work is defined as a behavior aiming at reducing biological tensions and safeguarding the organism's survival.[32]

But it seems artificial in most cases to draw a sharp distinction between play and work or between tension-seeking and tension-reducing behaviors. Obviously, when one unexpectedly meets a tiger on his way and then starts to run in order to escape, this act of running has no play in it; its sole purpose is that of reducing and eventually eliminating the person's fears in the face of the tiger. On the other hand, play itself can become a functional activity as when people turn games into a lucrative enterprise with the purpose of gaining money. Here, as in most ordinary activities, it is difficult to say where the playful activity of the imagination stops and where functional behavior begins. Also, play can be relaxing, not only tension-increasing and work can be aggravating, not only tension-decreasing.

We recall how the rats in Harlow's study chose to go the long way around a maze on their way to find food and this merely because of the interest associated with the more complex experience. Similarly, most human behaviors are not exclusively functional but also embellished with the arousing play of the imagination. On his way for a simple daily errand, a child or an adult might imagine himself as Joshua conquering the city of Jericho. Where does work stop and play begin in planning one's career? We embark on the course of becoming a father, a lawyer or a teacher but we leave a big part of these roles undefined and subject to our imagination. Although eager to acquire a *name* and thereby safeguard their survival, the people of Babel never chose a specific one. The cognitive Towers that determine a person's behavior and life do not resemble a complete construction. They always have unfilled gaps and undefined areas that arouse man's curiosity and give his creative imagination an opportunity to exercise itself.

We can then say that man is a playful union of the classic and the romantic. His classic activity is commonly tinted with romantic ambiguity or mystery and, on the other hand, his romantic aspirations can only express themselves against a classic background. The existential yo-yo game is this mixture of tension-reducing and tension-increasing activities, classic quiescence and romantic excitement during which man constantly erects as well as abandons Towers. And the emphasis is on the simultaneity of the process. We saw this union of opposites expressing itself in the attempt of painters to represent object identity, in the creation of religious movements, in the development of philosophical ideas or in the development of scientific theories.

Man's sanity depends on this constant interplay between the classic and the romantic. If his mind stops this play and becomes "serious," i.e., arrested either at the classic or romantic pole of cognition, it gradually loses its sanity. Therefore, both poles of human cognition, each with its opposing elements, may contribute to man's sanity and insanity.

The romantic flight from the center might be an indication of spontaneity, individual freedom and creativity. To become individual, idiosyncratic and non-conformist would then mean an actualization of human freedom which replaces old structures with freshly conceived forms of existence. But romantic adventures, whether in art, philosophy or politics also tear the individual from his haven, make him suffer the anxieties and guilt involved in asserting one's individuality while forsaking the original unity of his fellow artists, the family, the mother country or original culture. From this point of view, romantic aspirations might lead to the dispersion or loss of identity in colossal romantic revolutions. On the other hand, the classic pole of cognition has its own opposite aspects. A classic or unified view of the world could be obsolete, rigid and confining, but it could also be supportive and reassuring with its harmoniously balanced structure and the sense of identity it provides. Thus, unity and diversity, the two poles of the existential yo-yo game provide existence with two opposing meanings, each with its positive and negative elements. Sanity would depend on the constant interaction.

Interplay is then the definition of sanity, and one can find this definition looming already in Heracleitos' philosophy which views life as a perennial struggle of opposites, as well as in Schiller's theory concerning the play drive in man.[33] We can say that only sane people can play, or that sane is he who continues to play the yo-yo game of existence in which cognitive Towers organize the world, yet the identity of the latter is never completely formed or never receives a specific *name*. Again, play in this context means a mixture of functional, purposive activity and free, imaginative and non-functional behavior. In the following chapters we will see more specifically how the yo-yo game of existence is not one of "solitaire" but rather a social game. Like the jury that determines the reality of the crime, people play the existential yo-yo game together and determine for themselves how the universe looks and what is real and unreal, sane or insane. The identity of the universe is not something one "finds" but rather continuously creates with the help of other people.

CHAPTER 4

The Insanity of Not Having a Name

The trouble with insanity is that it is difficult to define. But this is the case with any identity, sane or insane. We must therefore study insanity in gradual steps, looking at it from one side and then from another until we form a notion of its nature, although it will continue to appear somewhat elusive.

By the term "insanity" we mean cognitive disturbances which are usually accompanied by emotional turmoil of many kinds.. We can generally divide these cognitive disturbances in two categories and therefore speak of two kinds of insanity. The one is the insanity of not having a *name* and the other is the insanity of having a *name*. In this chapter we will concentrate on the insanity of not having a *name*. Here the person's mind resembles the precarious existence of the people of Babel before they embarked on their monumental pursuit of an identity; the world is then devoid of unity, meaning and security. Like the people of Babel, the person without a *name* is afraid to be "scattered abroad upon the face of the whole earth."

We should first mention a heated debate in psychiatry on whether insanity or any mental disturbance is genetic, biological or, rather, the effect of an environment whose stresses can be overwhelming. On the one side of the controversy there stand Szasz and Mowrer, to mention two prominent representatives, who reject the concept of mental illness. What others would call a mental disease (in the sense that a flu or pneumonia is a disease), Szasz would consider merely an expression of "man's struggle with the problem of how he should live."[1] But there are other scientists like Eysenck who, although recognizing environmental stress as a factor in the development of a mental disorder, still emphasize its biological or genetic origin.[2]

The debate is often heated not because both parties have solid proofs of their arguments, but because the issue touches upon philosophical and moral values. In science, as in politics, value systems can override or dismiss the facts. For example, many scientists would revolt against genetic explanations of human behavior even before they paid them due attention mainly because racist ideologies heavily relied on genetics in the past. On the other hand, a moralist like Mowrer would reject the concept of mental disease merely because the acknowledgment of "sickness" frees the patient from the responsibility of his behavior. Instead, Mowrer ties mentally abnormal behavior with the concept of sin and considers mental patients responsible for their sinful (symptomatic) behavior.[3]

It is, however, impossible to dismiss the considerable and recent volume of research concerning the genetic origin of mental disorders.[4] By now it is a proven fact that the incidence of schizophrenia is higher among people who are genetically vulnerable to the disease. Also, Eysenck's claim that neurotic behaviors are biologically determined does not lack experimental basis. On the other hand, conceding this fact obviously does not exclude the possibility that environmental stress too may contribute to the development of a mental disorder.

No matter what the cause, a mental patient always finds himself in a cognitive and emotional crisis. His usual means of coping with life's problems have ceased to be effective. He cannot relate to people or respond to their demands. He is overwhelmed by anxiety or depression, incapable of "collecting" himself both emotionally and cognitively. Therefore, regardless of the specific organic components of mental disorders, they can all be defined by the cognitive condition of the patient involved.

Imagine yourself sitting in a big theatre filled with people listening to a speaker. Assume that for the sake of demonstrating a certain point, the speaker calls one person from the first row to come to the stage. Then, once the person reaches the stage, the speaker asks him to take two steps in front of the audience without explaining to him the purpose of the movement. Overwhelmed by this demand, as if he forgot how to walk, the person first looks at the speaker to ascertain that taking two steps is indeed what he is supposed to do, then he stares at the audience and back at the speaker. Desperately attempting to hide his anxiety behind a diffident smile, he finally moves his legs to take two sluggish steps. Somehow the smooth, unselfconscious nature of his habitual walking has disappeared and he now resembles a puppet mechanically moved by strings. Not only the audience notices this rigidity of the legs; he, too, is aware of the heaviness in the legs which seem reluctant to obey his wish to move. It is as if mind and body were separate somewhat, the former losing control over the latter.

Why did the legs lose their suppleness and vitality? It is because their required movements had no clear definition or meaning. In the past, every time this person walked, he knew why and whereto he was confidently striding; he was walking to his office or to his car. Some other time he was merely strolling along the banks of the river. In each case there was a meaningful context defining his movements and, therefore, they did not appear "out of place" or "unnatural." But now on the stage, only the speaker knows why he is to take two steps. And even if he were to know the purpose of the instruction to walk, he might still be ill-at-ease, inwardly embarrassed or anxious, out-wardly clumsy or rigid. It is most likely that the looks of the people in the audience would arouse in him this unnerving self-consciousness which eliminates smoothness, suppleness and liveliness from the body.

Sartre, as we shall see, considered the *look* a means by which a person makes his presence felt. I notice the existence of another person when I feel his look penetrating me through and through, introducing doubt, guilt, embarrassment or confusion in my soul. In the example we are now analyzing, the looks of the audience would fill the person on the stage with doubts as to the quality of his per-formance or the attractiveness of his body. Do they consider his body movements gross? Clumsy? Do they find him fat and ugly? Thus, even if he knew why he should walk, still he would not have a full grasp of his situation. He is no more the sole judge of his actions or the only person to provide meaning for his movements. With their penetrating looks, the spectators have become co-owners of his own legs since circumstances have permitted them to scrutinize these legs and pass judgment on their movements. His self-consciousness is then an appre-hensive awareness of what others might think or say. The looks have inserted a wedge of doubt between him and his body, or between him and his habitual walking movements. Thus, for a moment, this person loses full control over his own body as his legs grope for balance in a situation having no meaning or only an incomplete and vague defini-tion. He is at the mercy of the audience and the speaker who hide from him their judgment.

No one would characterize this momentary experience on the

stage as pathological or insane. Yet cognitively, *all* patients in a mental crisis undergo a similar experience and suffer from either a total lack of meaning in their existence or a partial eclipse of this meaning. The fact that they come to seek counseling or treatment in itself indicates that they are incapable of structuring their own lives meaningfully. Obviously they differ in the degree of their cognitive disorientation as well as in the intensity of their emotional turbulence. There is, on the one hand, the mild case where a patient displays a diffusive inadequacy in almost all aspects of his life. He does not know where he is heading, what career he should choose or how to ask his boss for a promotion. He experiences difficulty in finding friends or cannot adapt to his social environment. He therefore comes to a therapist, puzzled, confused or mildly depressed, asking for advice. There is, on the other hand, the neurotically anxious person, unduly concerned and agitated about many things, including trifles, yet not knowing what precisely causes his troubles or how to cope with them. Then there is the psychotic patient, suffering from confusion, perplexity, excitement, depression, bizarre thinking and "crazy" talk.

The official psychiatric nomenclature divides mental pathology into major divisions such as the psychoses, the neuroses, personality disorders, special symptoms, etc. And each division is itself differentiated into specific diagnoses. Clinicians know how difficult it is in daily practice to find the appropriate diagnosis for a patient, and very often patients are given three or four labels at once. For example, a patient might be labeled as suffering from "neurotic hysteria," "neurotic depression," and "social maladjustment" at one and the same time. There are also many vague labels like "adjustment reaction of adult life" or "occupational maladjustment" which presumably constitute "mental disorders." Besides the confusion that this multiplicity of names or labels often creates, it seldom has an absolutely valid meaning. Mischel has amply demonstrated how erroneous it is to believe in the existence of fixed traits of personality.[5]

The word "insanity," as we use it in this context, is a general term. It describes not only the highly disturbed people locked up in psychiatric wards, but every person who suffers from cognitive crisis or confusion, be it only for a moment, a week or a year. We all experience insane moments like the one on the stage described previously. Insanity is the lack of cognitive Towers or meaning that would organize our perceptions of the world into a sensible structure. The world appears then as patches of disparate colors, a pell mell of stimuli without substance or sense. It is only a question of intensity and duration of such an experience that would distinguish the "normal" from the "crazy" person. We can all afford brief moments of insanity without being considered "crazy." However, whether we deal with momentary or chronic insanity, the cognitive characteristics are more or less similar, differing in intensity and duration.

There are other universal features to the insanity of not having a *name* besides the cognitive confusion. In such insane moments, the world appears either infinitely slow or infinitely fast; consciousness becomes either a slow-motion picture or a vertigo. Recall those moments when you decided to go to the kitchen to bring a knife but you were distracted on your way by a phone call. Once you terminated the phone conversation, your legs continued to carry you to the kitchen yet you forgot what had brought you there. With glassy eyes, you looked at the objects around you, the stove, the table, the faucet, the pots. When your eyes encountered them, you did not understand why they were there at all; after all you were not looking for them. But because you did not know what you were looking for, the movement of your turning head or eyes became slower and slower, the objects you saw appeared more massive, bulkier and separate from one another. It is as if the tea pot no longer belonged to the stove, or the faucet to the sink. All objects were simply "there" without reason or meaning, slowly gravitating towards absolute rest. But then you remembered what had brought you to the kitchen and you quickly found the knife. Now on your way to it, all objects in the kitchen were suddenly "revived" and started to move again, each reoccupying the place where it belonged.

In a variety of degrees, all mental patients experience this slow-motion movement in consciousness in which objects almost come to a complete stagnation. Some patients stare vaguely into space with a detached look that sees practically nothing except static patches of colors or disparate figures hanging in the air. They later describe these moments as being "empty," the world appearing almost "hollow" or sparsely filled with objects that "do not go together." On the other hand, these patients may also experience vertiginous moments in which thoughts, words, objects, colors, madly race across in the mind. The extremely disturbed patient in a psychotic state literally sees the walls collapsing on him, the ceiling caving in, the windows flying in the air and he might then scream: "I am going to die, to die, something is going to happen, something terrible is going to happen." A less disorganized person would not hallucinate in this way, but would nevertheless experience emotional turmoil, anxiety and acceleration of thoughts. He is likely to say: "I don't know what is going on with me, please tell me what's going on, please, please . . . "

Meaninglessness or non-sense in the world can therefore be experienced either in a static or in an extremely speeded up and dizzying way. And in both cases meaninglessness fills the person with a sense of passivity and lack of control. It is with *names* or cognitive Towers that we organize our world, feeling "on top" of it. We know then where everything presumably belongs or what we are to do on this or that occasion, always being the "master of the situation." But without a *name* or identity, the universe becomes unpredictable, depriving people of all initiative. A person in a meaningless situation will feel passive, overpowered by events that "happen" to him and which he can neither understand nor control. This is the feeling of the person on the stage described earlier. He does not know why he has to take two steps, and he is therefore dependent on the guidance of the speaker or the gaze of the audience that scrutinize him. And like this person, many mental patients feel exposed to forces lying outside them, being at the mercy of powers that mechanically manipulate their movements as if they were puppets on a string. Sometimes they call these external powers "bad luck," "fate," "the devil," or "God." Asked what reason he had to believe that God indeed exists, one man in ancient Greece answered: "He hates me!"

Attributing inner confusion and emotional turmoil to the work of the devil, blaming fate for throwing the world into chaos, are desperate attempts many patients make to introduce method into madness. Much of the "crazy" talk of schizophrenics is known to be a direct effort to reconstitute the sense of reality or reorganize a collapsed world. But this effort is futile because it amounts to a hurried patchwork which momentarily "glues" the world together only to witness its disintegration again and again. In a sense, to blame the devil for the mind's confusion is to build a cognitive Tower with which the patient attempts to explain his predicament. However, this groping for external reasons for the vertigo and confusion usually intensifies the feeling of passivity and dependency within the patient. In these moments of distress and panic, it is, rather, an inner devil or fate that constantly haunts the patient's soul, reminding him of his vulnerability, helplessness and inertia.

Besides rendering the person passive, the insanity of not having a *name* separates his body from his soul, the first gradually coming to resemble a robot as the latter dissolves into abstract ideas and moods. Lost in his endless inner debate whether "to be or not to be," Hamlet complains of how "the native hue of resolution is sicklied over with the pale cast of thought." As the meaninglessness of existence becomes more predominant and the mind more immersed in abstract thought about spirits, fate or the devil, the body gradually loses its suppleness and freezes into robotlike existence. Obviously, the mechanical aspect of the body as well as the airy or abstract quality of the soul may appear in different degrees. There is sometimes the abstract-mindedness of a professor accompanied by the clumsiness of his body. Or there is the woman whose mind drifts in vague romantic dreams while her body is being used. And there are those moments of deep embarrassment or shame that flush the face, numb the body and confuse the soul. In an extreme crisis like catatonic schizophrenia, the patient may sit for days in one position, his body showing little flexibility as his eyes stare at nowhere and his mind is lost in space.

The separation between body and mind is better understood when its contrast, a lively union between body and soul, is noticed. Recall the graceful movements of ballet dancers. The dance itself is a set of rules that prescribe certain movements. Move to the left, move to the right, the legs are up and down, etc. Together with the music, these rules amount to a cognitive Tower aimed at organizing the dancer's movements in a certain way. When the dancer starts to practice his dance, in the beginning his movements are stiff and mechanical. But then as he lets the music and the rules of the dance "enter his legs," his body gradually loses its stiffness and overcomes its mechanical nature or materiality. It now moves swiftly and gently, as if gliding in the air. In graceful movements, such as the ballet dance, the gentle undulation of a walking cat or the slow fluttering of the bird's wings, body and mind, matter and energy, seem to form a single active entity.

To take another example, people who already know how to swim often wonder why others have difficulty in learning this skill. "It is so easy," they say, "all you have to do is to move your legs and this will keep you afloat." Obviously, by the time they learned to swim, they have absorbed, so to speak, through practice, the rules of swimming into their bodies. But for the beginner, swimming appears as an abstract skill. He may know the rules theoretically, or have even observed people swimming, but this is not enough to keep him from drowning. As long as swimming rules remain an abstraction in his mind, his body will appear heavy in the water, very likely to sink. It is the degree of abstraction in the mind that determines how mechanical or lifeless the body appears. And this is true not only in dancing, swimming or catatonic schizophrenia, but in all tasks or roles a person has to fulfill throughout life.

We saw that roles are cognitive Towers shaping man's life. To become a father, a woman, a politician or a lawyer would require a lifetime effort to satisfy the requirements as well as the expectations society has for such roles. Although roles, like any other identity, are elusive and there are various ways of being a priest or a teacher, society commonly draws the general outlines of roles in a relatively clear way and people more or less know what steps to take to play this or that role. As beginners they are, obviously, hesitant and clumsy in whatever they do but they soon learn the agility and adroitness of accomplished actors. In their own personal way, they perform in good faith the roles they have learned. When one of them claims he is a priest or a farmer, ordinarily there would be no reason to doubt his statement. He has already learned the characteristic gestures or life style that make a priest or a farmer, whatever these gestures are.

But what if the role is ambiguous, vague or too abstract to grasp? Then certainly the person trying to play it will appear stiff, affected, comical and untrustworthy. Society often creates phantom-roles that keep haunting people and demand fulfillment, although no one ever knows exactly what steps to take. For example, the phantom-role of the "intellectual." What makes an intellectual? Is it the number of authors one can quote? The number of times he uses the word "however" to build sophisticated statements? There have been various external manifestations of being intellectual, from the wearing of gold rimmed glasses to sporting raveled or patched up blue jeans, bearded face, disheveled hair, and expounding "liberal" comments.

But despite these apparent signs, the role of the intellectual remains vague, certainly more abstract than the roles of the musician or the carpenter. And the more abstract, phantom-like the role is, the further separated mind and body are, the former rarefied with vague ideas and the latter given to affected gestures.

There are many who are ill-suited for the role of the intellectual. They look for it in the concert hall even though they do not particularly like music, in art exhibitions although they may be bored to death or in fancy titles of books which they buy but never read. But it is like embracing a cloud; the phantom is nowhere. A young man pathetically discourses about "cultural revolutions," a young woman defends the cause of woman's liberation, but despite their earnestness there is something affected and artificial in their manner, often to the point of appearing ludicrous as a result of a dissolution between mind and body that makes these intellectuals *manqué* seem like mechanical puppets.

Indeed, the separation between mind and body often tends to be comic and to arouse laughter. For the comic, as Bergson shows,[6] is generated by a contrast between the lively and the stagnant, the spiritual and the mechanical. A clown stumbles and falls before our eyes and we burst into laughter. Here, the comic lies in the involuntary element of the fall. The human body, commonly perceived as energetic and elastic, is suddenly forced to freeze into a mechanical rigidity that makes it tumble like a string puppet. The human and the mechanical also appear in the child's behavior which is so often amusing and laughable. His body still uncoordinated, a three-year-old child lifts his finger to threaten a dog with a spanking but the people around start to smile and the dog finds the gesture unconvincing. Also laughable are the clumsy movements of some affable, absentminded professors and, generally speaking, any human behavior in which the mechanical movements are repeatedly displayed. For example, the repetitive jerky movements of clowns are comic and so are also many remarks and gestures of some psychotic patients.

But the separation between body and soul is not always comic. One is filled with pity, not laughter, when one sees the repetitive, jerky movements of a psychotic patient suffering from agitated catatonia. Also, we cannot continuously laugh at the affectation of an "intellectual" when we learn that this person has sacrificed many years of his life pursuing the "intellectual" phantom. Earlier we saw how momentary distractions, brief moments of cognitive confusion suffice to disorient and paralyze the body. Now there are people who have been forced to live in almost constant distraction or cognitive confusion, so that they have had no choice but to experience the continuous separation of body and mind. They have not been able to develop cognitive Towers to give their world meaning and identity. And even if they, nevertheless, have succeeded in forming some images of themselves or of the world, these images have remained vague, unreal and ghostly. It is as if they, too, were eternally standing on a stage before an audience, constantly exposed to the silent looks of the spectators while suffering the discomfort of an ambiguously defined or meaningless existence. Thus, what would give rise to the insanity of not having a *name* or identity is a constant exposure to ambiguity. It is the duration and intensity of ambiguity that would determine how insane people are, whether it is only for a few minutes, as is the case in momentary absentmindedness, or for life.

Mind-Shattering Ambiguity

What would be a clear and unequivocal phenomenon? One would say that an intense electrical shock is an example of an unequivocal phenomenon as it would always arouse feelings of acute pain. For the thirsty organism, water becomes an unequivocal stimulus because it quenches its thirst. The clearly painful or gratifying is easier to identify. We also know that the classic tendency of the human mind seeks to create unequivocal identities. However, in the ordinary environment, free from electrical shocks and other extreme disasters, objects tend to appear ambiguous. Although the water in the river and the fruits on a tree are in themselves gratifying, their location in an open field and the potential presence of an enemy often make them ambiguous, at the same time attracting the hungry animal and arousing its apprehension. Also, the darkness that falls upon nature, the mixture of shadows and lights, shed ambiguity and mystery over all objects as they partly hide, partly reveal their contours.

The ambiguous catches the attention because it commonly disrupts a normal course of action. The night is expected to be peaceful and calm and people then turn in to sleep. A sudden noise might simply arouse the curiosity of a sleeping person, alarm him or even amuse him. It would depend on how familiar or novel the noise is. There are different qualities to the ambiguous in existence and, as we shall see, it might either shatter or enrich man's mind. We should, however, remember that the ambiguous is not only a fortuitous event that befalls the organism; the latter actively looks for it even though it might sometimes be noxious or fatal. We saw that already at the second day of his life, a newborn infant will focus his attention longer on contours and contrasts of colors than on plain surfaces and would be likely to pay attention to his mother's eyes because of their black-white contrast. We all actively seek the puzzles, titillation, excitements and mystery offered by ambiguous, half-revealed, half-hidden objects.

The ambiguous is therefore seductive, as it is the nature of seduction to hide as well as reveal, to be on the one hand familiar, on the other hand mystifying, always promising more than giving. It is familiar enough to be reassuring, yet eccentric enough not to bore so that it remains attractive; but it attracts while imposing hindrances. This applies not only to sexual relations among people but also to spiritual or cognitive intercourse. Socrates was accused of the cognitive seduction and corruption of the youth of Athens by his philosophical sophistication. Later we shall also see how works of art or even scenes in nature might be seducing because of the ambiguity they convey. The question is when and how this seduction becomes harmful to man to the point of inducing insanity.

In his book *Aesthetics and Psychobiology,* Berlyne elaborates on the organism's need for arousal or tension increase.[7] He mentions surprises, complexity in phenomena, incongruity and conflict as "arousal increasing" stimuli that attract the organism. However, these arousing stimuli can be experienced as pleasurable only when the degree of arousal or titillation, so to speak, is not unduly high, causing aversion or pain. It is obvious, for example, that there is a limit beyond which a novel and sudden event cannot be considered a pleasurable but, rather, a painful surprise. Sometimes, this limit is not reached because the arousing stimulus is accompanied by another stimulus that neutralizes it, making it more gentle. Berlyne mentions music as an example where this combination of stimuli takes place. Whereas a contrasting combination of high and low musical tones might arouse the listener, a uniformity of presentation, as well as the rhythmic repetitions of tones, would have a calming effect on him. In this case the listener enjoys not only the pleasure of arousal engendered in him but also the pleasure of relief following an increase of tension. In other words, a good composer would know how to prevent the arousal his notes generate in the listener from becoming excessive by also using rhythmically lulling or soothing tones.

Nature too, displays this combination of stimulating and soothing effects. For example, whereas the weather generates arousal by its fast changes and surprises, the alternation of days and nights is rhythmic and repetitious, therefore reassuring as well as tension-reducing. Thus, two phenomena, the weather and alternation of nights and days occur at the same time, the one causing uncertainty and the other reassurance. One can be apprehensive about the kind of weather awaiting him in the morning but he at least knows that the morning will come for sure.

It would not be difficult to imagine the state of mind of a person exposed to a constant bombardment of conflicting stimuli, loud and confusing noises of all kinds, without experiencing anything calm or stable. It is as if he were constantly subjected to unruly weather without being reassured by the recurrent alternation of nights and days or the change of the seasons that would stabilize the weather. Indeed, many mental patients have been subjected since their early childhood to an environment where conflicting messages, unpredictable events and disrupted communications were not the exception but the rule. This is a kind of eternal ambiguity, madness without a method, that has prevented the classic tendency of the patient's mind from building a coherent image of the world or finding a *name* for existence. We are dealing here with a human environment in which people or families generate ambiguity to such an extent as to affect the patient's mind to the point of insanity.

Particularly interesting in this regard is Sartre's observation that we commonly feel the presence of other people through the ambiguity conveyed by their looks.[8] He makes the important distinction between the eyes of a person and his look. When a person looks at you, you can see his eyes but not his look. The look of the *other* is not an object that you can perceive but rather a feeling inside you, an undefined turmoil in your chest or stomach that makes you feel the presence of the *other*. Sartre gives the example of a person moved by jealousy, curiosity or vice who decides to glue his ear to the door and listen through a keyhole to a certain scene in a room. Suddenly another person passed in the corridor and looked at him listening or peeping through the keyhole. Obviously, if you were the person caught peeping, you would not *see* the look of the person that surprised you but only feel it inside you as a tormenting state of ambiguity. What is going to happen? Is the *other* going to inform the police? Is he going to tell all your friends about your disgraceful eavesdropping and peeping? You would not know the answers to these questions as you remain frozen beside the door.

For Sartre, then, human presence is felt through the ambiguity of their looks. It is the ambiguous and inscrutable look falling on you that tells you that the *other* exists outside your consciousness. You surely see many people around you, walking in the street, eating beside you in a restaurant or playing a football game. But, as such, they are merely objects in your field of vision and their act of eating or playing a football game in itself is not necessarily an indication of a human presence. After all, one could imagine robots eating in a restaurant or playing football. It is rather their ambiguous looks that disrupt your course of action or stream of consciousness, which make you feel their human presence. For Sartre, human beings first announce their presence through a disruptive ambiguity conveyed by their looks you do not see but only feel as they penetrate you from all directions, even when they come from behind. No other creature but man can look at you in this way, disrupting your inner peace and filling you with embarrassment and confusion.

However, Sartre's description is incomplete in the sense that human beings announce their presence not only through ambiguous messages but, as we shall later see, also through clear and unequivocal communications. But Sartre's observations are revealing since they accentuate the role of the *other* or the social environment in sending ambiguous messages capable of depriving the person receiving them from the sense of reality or, as Sartre puts it, "stealing" his world.

Human beings are highly skilled in delivering contradictory messages, saying "no" and "yes" at the same time. Man can affirm and deny, promise and recant, be serious and facetious simultaneously. He might answer "yes" to a question while at the same time twitching his nose and meaning "no." He can loudly say "sure, of course" while chuckling so that you would know he is not serious at all. Contradictory or ambiguous messages of this kind do not constitute a lie, for when one lies to others in a skilled manner, the unsuspecting listener would notice no contradiction or ambiguity in his words. Ambiguous communications, on the other hand, contain a riddle, a confusing element or a conspicuous incongruity that tangles the mind. Many studies done on the families of schizophrenic patients showed how these patients have been exposed at home to such ambiguous communication, which certainly aggravated their sickness.

One group of investigators focused on the *double bind* nature of conditions that prevailed at the home in which the schizophrenic patient grew up.[9] A double bind situation is one in which a person "can't win" no matter what he does. Each choice he makes is bound to make him appear guilty, as is the case when a mother buys two ties for her son on his birthday and, when he first wears one of them, she rebukingly asks: "What's the matter, don't you like the other one?" Now this is only a facetious example of a double bind situation but it certainly gives the flavor of the impasse in which the son is caught. What would he do? Wear the other tie? Then his mother would again rebuke him with the same question. Refusing to wear either one of them? This would certainly be interpreted as rejecting the mother's love and attention. And he obviously cannot wear both ties at once to satisfy her. Another double bind situation, more real and painful, would leave the son seething with anger, choking with rage yet incapable of confronting his mother with the injustice of her remarks as he is afraid of losing her love. Such is frequently the situation in the family of schizophrenics.

As another example, there is the mother who all along has rejected her son yet nevertheless expects him to give her a kiss when she comes to visit him in the hospital. Sensing her expectations, and being actually happy to see her, he extends his arms for an embrace. But then he feels her frozen body, the aloof expression on her face and the lack of warmth in her touch. On the one hand, he could not avoid giving her a kiss because in that case she would become angrier and more rejecting (What's the matter, don't you love me?). On the other hand, while embracing her he becomes aware of the cold expression on her face which makes him feel unwanted, as if he were doing something he was not supposed to do. No matter what decision he would make, he would be left with the bitter taste in the mouth that what he did "wasn't quite right" or that he should have done something else to satisfy his mother. Only, he would not know what this "something else" is or what would be the appropriate behavior in this case. Frequently caught in this kind of ambiguity and not knowing for sure what he should or should not do, he gradually loses his sense of reality.

A revealing description of ambiguous communications in a family is offered by Wynne:

The incident to be described from a conjoint family therapy session was characteristic of many that the family described as occurring in the past. The family consisted of the two parents, an 18-year-old daughter and a 16-year-old son who was the hospitalized presenting patient. He was a deeply perplexed schizoid young man who had, a year previously, pursued his mother with a butcher knife, but subsequently was unable to mobilize enough coordinated energy to continue in school or in private-office therapy.

After several months of family therapy, he had successfully resumed studying within the hospital setting and was making rather expansive plans for separating from his family as soon as possible. In this therapy session he was describing his wishes to hitch-hike between the hospital and home, as well as elsewhere. His father made an unusually active response and said explicitly that he did not want him to hitch-hike because this was too dangerous. He started to give examples of disasters that had befallen hitch-hikers. The son, and his sister who aligned with him, earnestly began to engage the father with counter-arguments.

Meanwhile, the mother was sitting silently but—and this is common in the concealment of meaning—with a broad smile that seemed to convey to the therapist (and to me, an observer through a one-way window): "I know all about this but am indulgently above such a childish dispute."

The other family members looked inquiringly at her and, after a bit, the father dropped the argument with his son and said rather plaintively to his wife, "I wish you'd tell us what you think, Mary Anne."

The mother merely chuckled and smiled more broadly. This brought forth an intense effort by each of the others, family members and therapist alike, to induce her to interact with them. They complained that they did not know what she was thinking and they needed her help. The mother then responded so softly that no one understood. When asked to repeat, she again merely smiled.

The father and son then slumped deeply into their chairs, apparently in despair, and the father said, "I'm talking down a blind alley."

After a short interval in which the therapist fruitlessly tried to intervene, Mr. B. again turned to his son and repeatedly spoke of the "reality" of hitch-hiking dangers. Just as the son started to revive and begin a vigorous response, Mrs. B. now spoke in clear, firm, and measured tones: "I am *aware* of reality but go *above* reality." The rest of the family, and the therapist, seemed too stunned to speak. The son collapsed into his chair and seemed preoccupied, in another world, and altogether withdrawn from further engagement with anyone. Implicitly, he and the other family members were agreeing and consensually validating a long-standing, shared family belief that mother had access to meanings on which the others were dependent—without which they could neither decide about, act upon, nor even sensibly discuss family controversies.[10]

The mother's supercilious smiles, her vague and mystifying remarks, the constant concealment of her real intentions could only intensify the feeling of dependency and helplessness in her son or in other family members. They might have to spend a lifetime in order to learn what she really thinks about hitch-hiking or other matters. But she would constantly resist committing herself by any clear statement, always remaining "above" the situation. And indeed, being ambiguous or noncommittal is one way of controlling people and remaining one up in the power hierarchy. Ambiguity attracts the attention, seduces the mind and immobilizes the body. In the example cited above, all family members were captive of equivocal messages which, like a magical spell, prevented them from making any decision or initiating any act. Having described the family interaction, Wynne adds that the mother deliberately intervened with such equivocal messages whenever she felt her son and husband were about to reach any agreement. To secure her way over her family she had to disrupt all liaisons among family members which might possibly lead to a "united front" against her. And she accomplished this task by the insertion of ambiguity in the conversation of others. We recall that when God decided to punish the people of Babel, He "confused their tongue" so that they could not continue their construction of the Tower or, symbolically, acquire identity.

In another family known to this writer, the father was the figure who "confused the tongue" of other family members. "In our family we all love one another." This was the father's usual response to his enraged youngest son, age ten, who constantly complained about his older brother. The latter was eighteen years old and had undergone an acute psychotic breakdown one year earlier. "But he was mean to me yesterday, picking on me, calling me names," screamed the young son. "No, you don't understand," replied the father, "he was just teasing you. I tell you he loves you!" Thus, while his son was seething with rage, the father was calmly trying to convince him that his feeling was "wrong" or unjustified since "we all love one another in the family." One seriously wonders whether the younger son would ever develop any stable sense of reality when his accurate perceptions are constantly and deliberately twisted or disconfirmed by his father. This father also used to repeat: "We are all equal in this family," basically meaning that no one could deviate from the standards of behavior he dictated at home. All family members were "equalized" before his throne. One of his rules was that no one in the family, not even his two daughters, would leave the door of any bedroom or of the bathroom locked when they were inside. "We don't have any secrets, do we? Besides, if you are in danger, I'd rather have your door open," he used to say. He also saw to it that his children exchanged their bedrooms in the house periodically, "so that no one becomes possessive and materialistic."

It was obvious that under the mask of democratic egalitarianism, this father was allowing no one to develop his privacy and individual life. Overtly, no one could complain as they were all treated equally. But this equality was experienced as the worst of all burdens, since it consistently blurred their individual self-image or identity. Most painful was the fact that the father usually avoided direct confrontation with any enraged family member. "Well, you know I always love you, don't you?" was his frequent response to complaints, and he uttered these words with a seductive voice, avoiding the real issue brought up by the complaint. To enforce his rules at home and correct deviant behaviors he would ask other family members, a son or a daughter, to rebuke or "straighten up" the person responsible for such behavior. Therefore, in the eyes of his children, his image presented a strange mixture between the saintly and the evil, but they would never know when he was the one or the other.

Haley shows how pathological symptoms are often themselves ambiguous messages containing an overt "yes" and a tacit "no" designed to control the relations with and behavior of another person.[11] Haley sees psychopathology as a paradoxical pattern of communication between two or more persons. And in each case of pathological relations, one person maneuvers, with the help of his symptoms, to circumscribe and control the other's behavior while indicating he is not doing so. For example, a wife might force her husband to take care of the house while simultaneously denying that *she* wants him to do so. She would claim, for example, that she has an allergy to soap, dizzy spells or other ailments that require her to lie down regularly. Thus, the wife is controlling her husband and forcing him to behave in a certain way while denying that *she* is doing this. After all, she cannot help her sickness. Obviously, faced with this paradoxical message, the husband will be equally ambiguous. He will clean the house but will somehow give his wife the message that *he* is not doing this out of choice and certainly not in response to *her* but only because of her pains that require this "involuntary" response from him. In this way the wife can never be sure whether her husband cleans the house because he loves her or whether she indeed has control over him. Being herself impersonal and ambiguous in her communications, she is bound to receive impersonal and ambiguous responses. Again, as Haley stressed, it is not pathological to gain control of the relationship with another person; we all do it. But when one attempts to gain that control while denying it, this is symptomatic behavior.

As Lidz shows, disturbed marital relations provide another kind of ambiguity which might adversely affect the sense of identity in the child. Many schizophrenic patients have parents who have suffered from marital discord which provided poor and ambiguous models of father and mother.[12] Constantly exposed to the disputes and fights between his parents, the pre-schizophrenic child could not develop any coherent awareness of roles he would fulfill in life. We saw earlier that being a man, woman, father or teacher is to undertake roles one has to perform throughout life. By modeling himself upon his parents and educators, a person learns to mold his life into this or that role, thereby acquiring the sense of who he is. But how can a child acquire a role of a man or a woman when he sees these roles at home being constantly criticized, devaluated, slandered or shattered to pieces by fighting between the parents?

"This you will never understand," said one wife condescendingly to her husband in front of this writer. She referred to a previous interview I had had with her concerning her son who was then hospitalized after a psychotic breakdown. In that interview I had suggested that after the son's discharge from the hospital he would need an extremely supportive attitude on the part of his parents. When the patient's father was also invited to an interview, his wife was communicating my opinions to him and then adding that he "could not understand them." It was obvious she was taking advantage of her son's condition to prove to her husband how unintelligent he was compared to her and to what extent he was responsible for their son's condition. She was a woman with intellectual aspirations that never materialized. Her husband was "only" a high school graduate whereas she "almost" finished college were it not for her "unexpected" preg-

nancy. Throughout the interview she was constantly trying to show
how open she was to "psychological issues," basically conveying to me
that she was on "my side . . . ." She derived an infinite satisfaction from
every talk she had with the physicians on the ward. It was as if her
son's hospitalization finally gave her the opportunity to associate with
people "to whom she belonged." However, when her husband heard
her condescending remarks, he dismissed her by saying: "You sound
just like your mother." She was desperately trying to sound "special"
and he was telling her she was only a "copy" of a model which he
already knew well.

This couple had been undercutting the worth of one another since
the first year of their marriage. Sexual relations were basically a battle.
In the beginning the wife did not sincerely admit her sexual needs,
fearing they might be interpreted as a sign of weakness. She would
therefore subdue much of her desires and when she enjoyed sexual
intercourse, she was careful to hide her satisfaction from her husband.
The latter, himself timid, naturally interpreted this as a rejection on
her part and started to blame her as being frigid. She responded by
claiming he was not a "real" man, following which he began to beat
her and to indulge in short love affairs occasionally. And this battle
extended itself to a competition for the loyalty of the children. "Your
mother is crazy," the father used to repeat to his son who later became
disturbed, "I am telling you she is crazy, don't believe a word she
says." The wife, on the other hand, used to cry on the shoulder of
this son, arousing his pity and anger while describing to him how
terribly painful his father's blows were and how she was trying her
best to please him although "he did not deserve it."

Themselves in need of support, the young children were forced
to take sides and buttress one or the other parent emotionally. In
their mutual undercutting, the parents could not serve as a coherent
model of a man or a woman, a father or a mother. Exposed to their
recriminations and slanders, the son did not know whether it is good
or bad to be a male or a father. And the daughter was totally confused
as to what "being a woman" means. "Don't be like your father,"
the mother would tell her son, also implying that being a male is in
itself undesirable since males only use, rape or beat women. The
daughter, too, would hear from her mother that men are "terrible"
and from her father that she should not be "empty-headed like her
mother." So both daughter and son were then totally perplexed as to

what they should become. Here they were, caught in a perennial battle between their parents, used by one side against the other, yet too young to understand the situation or defend themselves. For *any* child exposed to these conditions, the role of being a man or a woman would be difficult to grasp. He would live his entire life not knowing whether he should hate or love himself and, consequently, whether others can love him at all. The psychotic son of the family we mention here showed his first signs of depression and withdrawal at the age of puberty. He was ashamed of his sexual desires, terrified at the possibility that he, too, would be a "sex maniac" like his father. He later developed homosexual tendencies which further exacerbated his depression and at the end, just before his breakdown, he was thinking of committing suicide. Thus, we have a case of progressive ambiguity beginning with the unclear models of parents, then the son's bewilderment as to what he was, male or female, and last his wish to die, telling his therapist that death is the only place where one can be "nobody" without feeling guilty about it.

Regardless of the specific kind or origin of traumatic ambiguity, its victim is always filled with the sense of being an object, used and abused without his consent, yet feeling guilty as if he were the one responsible for his condition. Whether the ambiguity is reflected in an inscrutable and embarrassing look, in a double bind communication leading to an intolerable dilemma, in vague and mystifying smiles or remarks or in the role confusion at home—in all these cases, the person feels overwhelmed by forces he can neither understand nor control. Here we should again recall the different representations of object identity in painting. We saw that in romantic trends of art, the relations between the object and its environment can be over-stressed, sometimes to a point where the object loses its legibility. In such instances the environment penetrates the object from all directions, and the latter dissolves, so to speak, in the relations it maintains with other objects. Such is also the case with the schizophrenic mind that loses its boundaries and yields to overpowering forces sweeping it from the outside. It is impossible to develop firm ego boundaries or acquire a relatively distinct identity when one is constantly bombarded with ambiguous messages, blurred models of roles or penetrating and embarrassing looks. Faced with ambiguity, the classic tendency of the mind is hampered in its role of establishing a relatively unified and distinct awareness of the world.

A clear indication of this invasion of a person's mind by the environment is the *overinclusive* thinking of many schizophrenics.[13] They can "squeeze" together various and irrelevant perceptions in one concept or include different and contradictory thoughts in one sentence:

> I need a dumptruck to unload my head—(Moses, Jesus— don't follow leaders, watch parking meters)—You are God, World, 1974. Be a brother, help I need somebody. Acquire a peace of mind, turn your radio off! Can't find my way home.

One can still find some sense in this "word salad" uttered by a schizophrenic patient. The patient says he is overloaded with thoughts and is yearning for peace of mind. He betrays his revolt against authority figures ("Don't follow leaders!") as well as the fact that he feels guilty and afraid of authority (watch parking meters). However, his utterance is a pell mell of various thoughts which often would not make any sense to the listener. A patient might hate, for example, his domineering father and include in the concept of "father" all people who wear hats since his father wears one. Then he would hate all hats, identifying them with the authority he dislikes so much yet is profoundly afraid of, to the point of believing it is God Almighty. He might therefore say: "Hat, Hat Almighty, please help me!" Frequently, this condensation of concepts contains highly symbolical meaning, as the objects of which the patient thinks lose their boundaries or fuse unrecognizably with other objects. And with this bewildering criss-crossing of thoughts and concepts, the patient feels overpowered and exhausted: "Help, I need somebody."

This feeling of helplessness usually makes the patient meek and compliant. Enmeshed in the ambiguous messages he receives as well as in his own "word salad," he is incapable of making any decision and prefers to comply with what people order him to do, either directly or subtly. But there are moments when the feeling of being used as an object enrages the patient and he then acts out his fury in disorderly behavior, "crazy" temper tantrum and assaultive conduct. Destruction seems to him the best way of asserting himself and tasting the flavor of freedom. He feels then he can challenge everybody, including his father, mother and God. But these are usually short-lived episodes or "breakdowns," followed by intense pangs of shame and guilt which exacerbate the patient's depression.

At other times, the patient will try to acquire identity as well as the sense of independence by joining a group and borrowing its *name*. So he becomes, almost overnight, an ardent believer in Zen, a convert to the Jewish or Moslem faith or a loyal member of a group with a glamorous name, such as "The Task Force of Christ" or "The Anti-Satan League." This would be a desperate attempt to purchase quickly a cognitive Tower which could give meaning to his existence. However, this would be a borrowed Tower which, like a borrowed suit, is either too long or too short, rendering its wearer incongruous, even comical. Earlier we gave the example of the accomplished ballet dancer who has already absorbed into her body the rules both of the dance and the music. She therefore appears to be almost gliding in the air when she performs her role, her graceful body seemingly having entirely lost its physical qualities of weight and mass. But when the rules of the dance are still abstract, i.e., not yet absorbed by the body, the latter may appear mechanical and at times comical like a puppet moved by strings. Such, in most cases is the picture of the person suffering from the insanity of not having a *name*. He drifts through life, borrowing identities from this or that group to hide the "nobody" which he feels inside and of which he is so ashamed. But whatever he picks up as a *name* only emphasizes the "nobody" in him, sometimes pathetically. For then he is like an engine that works by fits and starts. Today he wears this badge, tomorrow another label and the next day yet another *name* until a psychotic breakdown or suicide provides a convenient escape.

We have thus far listed several types of ambiguity capable of shattering a person's mind and inducing insanity. We expanded on schizophrenic patients as victims of ambiguous environments. However, not every person exposed to double bind communication, to marital discord between his parents or to ambiguous looks necessarily becomes schizophrenic. We said at the beginning of this chapter that the word "insanity" as we use it in this context describes not only the highly disturbed people in locked wards, but every person suffering from cognitive confusion, be it momentary or chronic. Therefore, people differ in the degree of their "insanity" depending on the duration and intensity of the ambiguity they have been exposed to. Some suffer only momentary confusion or absentmindedness, others are chronically perplexed and dependent most of their lives and still others become psychotic.

Too, the degree of mental disturbance or the intensity of the insanity of not having a *name* is determined not only by environmental factors such as ambiguous messages but apparently also by biological deficiencies with which people are born. The role that biological factors play in the human mind is becoming more conspicuous as research progresses. As Pavlov, and later Eysenck, showed, people differ in the degree of cortical arousal which in turn determines how fast and firmly they learn from their experience. To a large extent, biological factors determine how lucid or ambiguous, logically coherent or "fuzzy" a person's mind is. Depending on whether they are born with a high or low degree of emotionality, or whether they are extravert or introvert by nature, people will differ in their tendency to construct cognitive systems or acquire a *name* for themselves. One person will construct a cognitive Tower quickly, another slowly. One will develop, like the obsessive-compulsive person, a highly complex belief system that pervades his entire existence and guides his behavior. The other, like the hysteric, will construct small and shaky Towers, frequently abandoned and easily replaced.

Genetic or biological factors also play an important role in the development of schizophrenia. It has been repeatedly claimed that schizophrenic patients suffer from impairment in their sensory perception due to a biological deficiency.[14] An overactivity in the reticular formation of the brain or other disturbances in the central nervous system might disrupt the patient's perception and muddle his mind. He might not have the selective perception or "filter mechanism" that normal people have and would therefore perceive too much, see more than others, his mind being constantly flooded with stimuli which he cannot possibly organize coherently. Or he might perceive too little, being blind to essential details in the environment while listening to inner "noises" originating in his own organism. He cannot build a relatively coherent or "sane" picture of his existence as his mind is overcome and distracted by the bombardment of stimuli.

It is then reasonable to assume that both environmental and biological factors coalesce in inducing the insanity of not having a *name*. The genetic make-up or a certain biological lack, coupled with an ambiguous environment, would, in varying degrees, prevent the classical tendency in the mind from building a relatively coherent image of the world.

CHAPTER 5

The Insanity of Having a Name

We said earlier that in so far as mental disturbances are considered along a cognitive dimension, they can all be divided into two patterns which we call the insanity of not having and the insanity of having a *name.* In the last chapter we concentrated on the pathology of not having a *name,* or the cognitive confusion characteristic, in various degrees, of all patients seeking therapy. Here we shall discuss the second pattern of insanity, that of having a *name,* which commonly accompanies the first pattern described.

We saw that the people of Babel looked for a *name* yet they were reluctant to choose a *specific* one. They searched for an identity but they also dreaded its final acquisition which resembles in many ways the finality of death. For, in a sense, only dead people possess finished and fixed identities, since they are no longer capable of redefining themselves. To have a fixed *name* is to confine identity, narrow its scope and arrest its growth. Being alive, the people of Babel were defining and redefining the meaning of their unity, enacting and then amending social laws, specifying and then changing daily goals. They resisted established norms and unchangeable *names* and it was only after they had been dispersed that a *name* was given to their unity. Similarly, every strong conviction or "truth" about oneself, others or the world casts identities in rigid molds. For names, labels, images or other concrete representations of any identity reveal only some of its facets, leaving the rest untouched and undisclosed. When man's cognition becomes entrenched in adamant convictions and totally occupied by *names* about every matter in the world, it loses the resilience necessary for coping and surviving in a constantly changing world.

Bewildered, overwhelmed or panic-stricken as patients may seem, they rarely display a prolonged or total intellectual stupor. Their

81

cognition is not wholly shattered, for along with their bewilderment
they also express convictions in regard to their crisis, offering definitions or a *name* with which they explain their situation. The acute
schizophrenic, for example, does not display only confusion, perplexity and emotional turmoil indicative of the shattering ambiguity he has
been exposed to in his life. He also develops convictions to explain his
world, cognitive Towers to provide meaning for his existence. The
classic tendency of his mind is not entirely paralyzed, and it continues
its attempt to structure his experience. "God is speaking to me, I hear
the Voice, the Voice, the Voice," repeated one patient. Another would
attribute his inner turmoil to the work of the devil: "Satan, may God
wipe out his name, made me suffer. I am afraid of Satan!" Yet another
patient would attribute his troubles to unknown magnetic forces emer-
ging from the T.V. set or from the moon. Bizarre as these delusions
may seem, they are *names* with which the patients attempt to put method
in the madness and to structure their world.

Or take the manic-depressive patient as another example. On
the one hand he experiences periods of extreme elation, irritability,
non-stop talkativeness, and acceleration of speech and ideas. He ram-
bles from topic to topic, being as confused about the one as about the
other. But then this unstructured or "fluid" state of mind might be
replaced by a gloominess and absolute conviction about imminent
disasters and death. He would insist, for example, that this world is the
worst of all possible worlds, that it is, like Sodom and Gomorrah,
doomed for destruction because it is filled with vice and sin. For him,
then, evil is the true identity of this world.

A less disturbed person, like the obsessive-compulsive neurotic,
will also display this cognitive mixture of, on the one hand, perplexity or indecisiveness and, on the other hand, rigid convictions and
ritualistic behavior. He will vacillate between possibilities or opinions,
endlessly weighing the pros and cons of a certain decision without ever
making it. "Should I do this? Maybe I shouldn't! However, I have to.
But . . . ," and so forth endlessly. He cannot get rid of these recurrent
ideas, his sleep is disturbed and he worries constantly. But, too, he
will entertain various convictions with the persistency and stubbornness
of a mule. Certain things must be done only in one way or else he
will think the sky is falling. "Son, I am telling you, two and two are
four," he will repeat to emphasize the "truth" of his convictions as
to what people should or should not do in a particular case. Thus,

despite his vacillation in some matters, he attaches many fixed *names* to his world.

In one way or another, all patients develop identities which they consider, either rightly or mistakenly, the "cause" or the "nature" of their emotional and cognitive confusion. Anything from God and the Devil to "bad luck" or the parents might serve as the explanation or meaning of their predicament. However, the patients' convictions are often inappropriate, mistaken, unlikely to square with experience or incapable of alleviating their emotional pain. So they swing from the state of having a *name* or some definition of their condition back to a state of confusion or lack of a *name*. The cognitive Towers they construct are too narrow, shaky or rigid to sustain the vicissitudes of life. They finally ask the therapist for the explanation and the cure of their troubles.

We should stress that it is not the *need* to coin a *name* for his existence that makes the person insane. *All* people, sane or insane need and find *names* for their existence. We saw earlier while discussing schools of art, philosophy and science, that "objective reality" is not a given fact one "finds" in the world. It is always a cognitive belief —be it mythical or scientific— that introduces "reality" into existence and therefore creates a cosmos or a world as an organized and meaningful whole. We also said that only in so far as man is capable of giving an identity or a *name* to his world can he also acquire self-identity. Beliefs about the world determine the person's behavior and therefore his self-identity. For example, your identity is different from mine, because you believe that this world is good and reflect this belief in your cheerful mood, in the enterprises you embark on, in your decision to get married and raise children, etc. On the other hand, I believe that this world is bad, so I do not marry or raise children; I do not embark on big projects and I do not trust people. Thus, every person needs to coin a *name* for his world so that he acquires certain roles and behaviors to distinguish him as a separate identity.

This explains why people, including patients, are reluctant to relinquish or change their convictions or beliefs. To renounce convictions is to lose the only expression man has of self-identity. Even when a patient develops strange delusions, such that ghosts are coming from the moon to rule the world from T.V. sets, he thereby builds a world for himself and acquires his own distinction. Although other people might not share these convictions, they do provide him with an identity. He is not a "nobody." He is a particular individual, *different* from others because he has these convictions. They make him special or even unique. People recognize him by his ideas: "This sounds like him," they will say. He will therefore be proud of his ideas, strange as they may seem to the observer, and would not renounce them easily. Sometimes he might even say: "I am crazy, you know," meaning he has his own independent mind.

Furthermore, to have a conviction or a belief is to have power. He who defines a situation, in a sense controls it. Since "objective reality" is not a given fact but rather an identity born of beliefs, man, the inventor of *names*, enjoys the feeling of superiority, power and mastery each time he coins an identity or creates a reality. Each time he says: I believe that so and so . . ., an identity is created and confirmed in the world. We recall the sexual symbolism conveyed by the story about the Tower of Babel. Like a procreative act, the erection of cognitive Towers or the coining of *names* brings to the world new identities. And it is this role of a creator and master that man assumes each time he develops or reaffirms a conviction. "I believe the world is flat," "I believe the world is round," "I think my neighbor is wicked," "My wife is great but her mother is intolerable," etc. Whether in mere gossip or in more serious philosophical thinking, man elevates himself to the role of a master when he imposes labels on his environment.

It requires strength and determination—we called it positive aggression—to shape the world according to this or that belief. One needs courage to declare: "I believe . . .," the boldness to impose his own views on the world. Therefore, asking a person to renounce his convictions—bizarre as they may seem to the observer—would be challenging him to lose power or supremacy over his world and thereby his own identity. Obviously, he would resist and jealously guard his possession.

Therefore, it is not the having of a *name* that spells insanity but only the having of a *specific* one, something which the people of Babel avoided. It is precisely in creating identities in the world and finding meaning in his universe through the construction of cognitive Towers that man manifests his mental vitality, his creativity as well as his self-identity. But when *names* are considered final and fixed and man says: "The world is *only* this and that," then thinking begins to show signs of rigidity or pathology. Man seems then to forget the main characteristic of all cognitive identities, namely, the elusiveness of these identities which tend to crystallize and dissolve as a recurrent process. Healthy cognition interacts with its environment, constantly redefining or changing its concepts while molding reality. Unhealthy cognition, on the other hand, tends to confine itself and, therefore, the world, to fixed *names*.

An identity is born in relation or in contrast to other identities. One determines the cold in relation to the hot, the beautiful in contrast to the ugly, and the wise in contrast to the foolish. For example, if I decide to regard myself a wise person, I am never wise alone, by myself, but always in relation to my friends, rivals or enemies whom I consider wiser or less wise than I. Even if I secretly believe that I am the wisest, the richest and most powerful among people, I continue to invite people for tea or cocktail parties for it is only in their presence that I can reaffirm or taste, so to speak, my own wisdom, riches or strength. Hence, I depend on people to nourish in me the feeling of being wise or powerful. And it is in this contrast between my wisdom and theirs, my wit and their wit that I can feel how different I am; I am a separate identity who is wiser or less wise, richer or poorer, more or less handsome than they. Whatever *name* a human being has, whether it is being tall, short, handsome or pleasant, this *name* is coined in relation or in contrast to other *names*. History has known many thinkers who, like Plato, believed that there exist absolute norms of beauty, wisdom, perfection, etc. But these supposedly absolute norms are abstract ideas without basis in reality. The human mind cannot conceive any identity except through relations to other identities.

And in this commerce among identities, they all affect and help shape one another. Open-minded people learn from one another. Yes, I want to be the wisest among my rivals, but then I must constantly enrich my mind with other points of view which I can learn only from them. To illustrate, I cannot see this chair from all angles at once. I do not know how I myself look. I must therefore learn from others how this chair, this table or the moon looks "from the other side." We saw that an identity awareness of an object evolves when its various angles, aspects or points of view are simultaneously coordinated and woven into one unity. But this is an endless process because sane identities are always in the making and, as long as I live and, hopefully, maintain a healthy cognition, I continue to depend on other people to enrich my cognition and make it grow. And I depend on every one, on wise and foolish rivals, on friends and foes, on the young and the old. From the wise I learn how to be, and from the foolish I learn how not to be. My enemy would teach me a point of view and my friend would confirm or correct the ones I already have. When I finally recognize this dependency on other people, I become, if not more humble, then at least less resentful.

Assimilation and accommodation—this is how Piaget termed the healthy process of cognitive development. We cruise through life, trying to adapt ourselves to our environment and survive. We assimilate what we encounter along the way into what we already know, as well as accommodate ourselves to the environment. If we indeed possess a healthy mind, we must change our concepts and ideas to adjust to new phenomena which come our way. This means that throughout life we are half-active, half-passive; we act upon and change our environment but we also let it change us. While describing, in the previous chapter, the insanity of not having a *name,* we emphasized the passivity it entails for the patient. Faced with a mind-shattering ambiguity, the patient gradually gives in to forces manipulating and controlling him from the outside. He gradually comes to resemble an object, losing all initiative in life. On the other hand, in the insanity of having a *name,* the patient stubbornly strives to remain powerful and in control in spite of circumstances that prescribe an opposite approach. This is a desperate attempt to be always active, never passive, ever independent, never dependent. The patient will therefore resist free commerce with other identities in his environment, or avoid an open exchange of points of view. He will want to assimilate his environment to his domain of power and under his control. Only his Tower should scrape the sky, dominating others—so he believes. However, what he does not realize is the fact that he is a prisoner in his own Tower, a slave to the rigidity of his mind and the uniformity of his behavior.

Many examples of the insanity of having a *name* can be cited, and we will first mention the people of Sodom and Gomorrah. The Biblical tale relates that "the men of Sodom were wicked, great sinners against the Lord." So God decided to send two angels to examine the moral condition of the cities and destroy them if indeed evil was rampant there. The two angels came to Sodom in the evening and Lot, who was a righteous man, saw them first as he was sitting at the gate of the city. He immediately rose to meet them "and bowed himself with his face to the earth," according to an Oriental custom of receiving guests. He did not know their mission, or suspect their intentions. With wholehearted generosity he invited them to spend the night in his house "and he made them a feast, and baked unleavened bread, and they ate."

But the men of Sodom, "both young and old, all the people to the last man, surrounded the house." Loudly and persistently this mob shouted at Lot: "Where are the men who came to you tonight? Bring them out to us, that we may know them." In Hebrew, the verb "to know" also means to possess sexually, as in the expression: "Adam knew Eve." Thus, the people of Babel wanted to rape the two angels. They did not rush to Lot's house to welcome the guests, acknowledging their right to be different and trying to learn what news they brought with them. Instead, they rushed to Lot's house to absorb or assimilate the guests into their existing pattern of life and thereby blur the presence of something different, although perhaps better or wiser. The Sodomites had already acquired a specific *name,* a definite behavior and a philosophy of life to which they were already absolutely committed. Hence, they could not tolerate newcomers, foreigners who might have a new value system, a different *name* that would challenge their fixed identity. In fact, Lot himself was an alien who had only recently settled in their city. Therefore, when he tried to dissuade them from raping his guests (he even offered his daughters instead) the Sodomites answered: "Stand back! This fellow came to sojourn, and he would play the judge! Now we will deal worse with you than with them."

Not willing to accommodate the newcomers in their city, the Sodomites lost their lives. Had they treated the angels with respect, wondered about their visit and asked them about their mission, they could have been saved. In Piaget's language, a cognition that only assimilates without accommodating itself to a new and changing environment is unadaptive and bound to perish. When Lot finally learned about the angel's decision to destroy the city, he rushed to tell his sons-in-law so that they could leave the city in time. But his sons-in-law thought he was jesting. They, too, could not see beyond the narrow limits of their life routines, could not believe that there are often changes in the world to which one should adapt. They had enjoyed that false sense of eternity characteristic of fixed habits and stagnant life. So they perished.

And Lot's wife perished too. She became a pillar of salt. The angels took Lot, his wife and their two daughters by the hand and brought them outside the city before destroying it. They asked them not to look back, but only forward, towards a new life and a new place. In this sense, the angels were essentially asking Lot's family to make changes in their identity or in their *name*. But Lot's wife looked back as if to relocate herself in the beaten tracks of her familiar town. Hence she was trapped in her habitual identity, shrivelled and frozen in her old *name*.

The insanity of having a *name* is this very imprisonment in a single life style, in one philosophy or in a fixed identity. And the major feature of such an insane mind is the way it "knows." Like the Sodomites, the insanity of having a *name* seeks to assimilate whatever it encounters to its own frame of reference, never truly recognizing or acknowledging any new fact. In this sense, to "know" is not to learn something new but rather to subjugate the new to the old. Hence the wish of the Sodomites to rape Lot's guests is the ultimate disregard for privacy or independence. And this is true not only of physical rape but also of cognitive rape. To assert its control over its environment, the mind locked into one belief will constantly attempt to demean, subjugate or rape other minds within its environment.

Take the case of Mr. M., a 57-year-old white man, father of two sons and one daughter. Mr. M. was hospitalized in the psychiatric ward after he had. exploded at work, hitting and injuring a black worker. No similar incident had occurred in the past and Mr. M. was known as the most industrious, punctual and loyal employee in the company. His violent behavior came as a shock to all his colleagues who had to subdue and rush him to the hospital. When he first arrived in the ward, he burst into tears and cried bitterly. Later he became progressively more depressed and on the fourth day of his hospitalization, he was found dead. He had hanged himself in the shower room.

When I interviewed him, he first spoke about his daughter, who is the eldest, then about his youngest son, calling both "good-for-nothing." About the incident at work he talked little but instead rambled on about the loose morals of the "young generation." He wept when he described how hard he worked to raise up "good children," sending them to college so that they would acquire "a good education." However, all three children dropped out of school. The daughter ran away from home with a black man, the youngest son joined a commune and was apprehended by the police because of drug abuse. The middle one preferred to stay home with his parents, "idling and sleeping all day," as his father said.

Although bitter, frustrated and depressed, Mr. M. expressed himself forcefully in every therapy session, hardly allowing me to interject any remark. Also, he frequently rose from his bed, looked at me from above as I was sitting on a chair and, while pointing his finger at me, he would repeat: "You doctors don't know how I feel! You think I am crazy, don't you? Well I am telling you, this damn world is crazy, not me!" It was obvious that he was trying to control the entire session, either by his continuous speech or by his occasional bursts into tears during which all conversation had to stop. And there was something touching in the way he expressed himself. He was a tall and solid man, a lawyer by education. In the hospital, he insisted on wearing his suit with a pocket watch looming from the vest. While pleading his case before me, one could see he was desperately battling against the evident helplessness which he felt in regard to his rebellious children. But he would not admit his defeat. He also chose to die in this suit, clinging to his identity to the end.

In the second day of his hospitalization I convened the family to discuss the case while the father was present. The patient's wife appeared meek, submissive and hardly spoke a word. But the air grew heated as the patient and his daughter immediately clashed in a loud dispute. Apparently, on the evening before the incident at work took place, the daughter had come with her black boy friend to visit her mother for the first time since she left home. "You came on purpose to make me mad," shouted the father during the family session. "No, I only wanted to see mother," replied the daughter. "Why then did you bring your black boy friend with you? You wanted to make me mad! I am not stupid, you know," retorted the patient. "Damn it," shouted the daughter, "why can't you listen to me just once? Listen to me! Why do you always have to put ideas in my mind which I never thought of?"

And indeed it appeared that the father had always imposed himself on the family as a "mind reader," a role which all the children came to hate intensely. When he was a student in college, he attended a few courses on psychology and was enthralled by Freud's theory which taught him the sophistication of going behind appearances to

determine the "real" meaning underlying what is said or unsaid. Therefore, he would hardly take anything said at home at its face value.
On many occasions he would find it difficult to believe that his children really meant what they said, and he was therefore keen on interpreting to them what their words or behavior "truly" meant. "When
I was ten years old," complained the daughter in the session, "he
started to teach me this junk about Freud. Whenever I had a quarrel
with my mother because she wouldn't let me do something I wanted,
he would say that I was angry at her because, *actually,* she was my
sexual rival for his love. And when I was seventeen and started to
date one guy at school, he became outraged and said that I could not
love a guy like him, that I only *thought* I was in love, and that I did
that only to free myself from the Oedipus complex in a very quick
and cheap way." "With my father," added the youngest son, "you
can never win!"

This insatiable need to read or invade the minds of his children
was equivalent to a physical rape. For Mr. M. showed hardly any
respect for his children's feelings. "Don't tell me how to handle a
child," he used to brag. Beneath his mask of a modern, liberal father,
Mr. M. was essentially a prejudiced despot constantly in fear of losing
his throne. But his children revolted against him, each in his or her
particular way, and in the last three or four years he became aware
he was losing ground at work, too. People became increasingly polite
to him, frequently excusing themselves from his presence to escape
his moralizing harangues. Especially resentful toward his daughter who
was dating a black man, he finally vented his rage against the black
worker, who supposedly was impolite to him. Mr. M. had to maintain
his control over people at all costs. He always had to feel strong,
wise, independent and master of any situation. So when he realized
that things were not the way he wanted them to be, he decided to
commit suicide. And one would say that even in this act he wished
to prove his power. It is as if he told God: "You want to make me
miserable, you want to kill me? Thank you, but I can kill myself!"

We can find around us not only one Mr. M. but many, symbolized
by a Batman, a Superman or a John Wayne. John Wayne (the film
character, not the person) is powerfully masculine, at ease in surmount-
ing hurdles or in saving himself or others from any of life's predicaments. He hardly finishes one mission before he sets out upon
another. He is a perpetual achiever who never fails, a good Samaritan

who hardly tarries to hear the expressions of gratitude or love lavished on him by those he helped or saved. He has no time for such "childish sentimentality." You do not see him crying, of course, for crying is a form of weakness unbecoming to men. In a sense he is eternal, solid as a rock, constantly challenging fate with his crooked smile, and his few words confidently uttered through the side of his mouth. In life there are many imitators of this strong silent type but the question is whether this role, even if it were attainable, is desirable. Does being strong always guarantee health and survival? No, for sometimes it is disastrous.

When young children become physically sick, they slow their activity, withdraw to a corner and rest or sleep. A wounded animal stops fighting and crawls into a niche to lick its wounds. This withdrawal is an admission of weakness, an acceptance of defeat which eventually helps the organism to recover. Whereas children readily show their dependence on cuddling, nurturing and love which helps them to overcome their illness, adults often play the role of independent heroes. They can work despite the flu! However, the flu may develop into bronchitis, the bronchitis into pneumonia and the person may soon find himself confined to bed, more in need of nursing than an infant. Had he admitted to his feeling sick and stayed at home to be treated, he would have spared himself his total dependency on others when incapacitated by pneumonia. This is to say that admission to weakness or acceptance of the role of being dependent may be as essential to survival as the role of being strong. However, some patients refuse to be dependent. But, unlike John Wayne who somehow manages to remain eternal, they are more likely to die.

This vanity is more common to mental than physical sickness. One of the major difficulties therapists experience with patients is the refusal of the latter to recognize any weakness in themselves. It is true they come to seek help, to ask the therapist for good advice. But they soon try to turn the therapy sessions into a tribunal and the therapist into a judge in front of whom they plead "not guilty" while blaming the entire world for their misery. The husband will blame the wife and the wife will blame her children while the latter shrug their shoulders and blame fate or God. Despite their explicit demand for help and their promise to change whatever is needed in order to improve, patients often tend to cling to their beliefs, even enter into a heated discussion with the therapist to prove how right they are. A typical example of this resistance to change is the following case.

Mr. T. was a 45-year-old school principal who was referred to me by his physician because of his chronic hypertension. It was felt that psychotherapy and relaxation exercises might be helpful in reducing his anxiety, make him ease up his frenetic life style and hopefully control his elevated blood pressure.

He was short, slightly overweight and did not look attractive in his grayish, almost colorless suit which he wore every time I saw him. In the first session he was obviously tense, constantly fidgeting on his chair or crossing his legs, rhythmically shaking the foot on top of his knee while tapping the shoe with his finger. "What do you think, sir?" he repeatedly asked while describing his troubles with his wife at home as well as the pressure of work at school. "Do you think I should have done that? What do you think, sir?" At times he would pull his chair as close as possible to the desk and lower his voice: "Well, you know how it is with the wife. You do have a wife, don't you?" To see him speaking to me in this way, one would say he was offering to connive with me against the devil, and this after intimating that we both might have the same problem. After all, we both are men and "*we* know how troublesome wives can be." It was clear that, following the initial moments of acquaintance during which he was polite and respectful, Mr. T. was trying to tell me that we were equal in status, intelligence and possibly in misery, as we were both married.

Overtly, Mr. T. was not playing the role of John Wayne, or of Mr. M. whom we described above as one who wished to gain power by directly imposing his will on others. He could not assume this role openly as he lacked the charm which usually makes words sound more convincing. Nevertheless, he was hungry for power and control over people. He did not try to gain this control by stating a point of view that would attract people because he had no personal point of view. He would not commit himself directly and affirmatively to any philosophy or code of behavior. Instead, he would assert himself by constantly finding flaws in others. He was the type of person who would read a book not to learn from its contents but to look for typographical errors. In his conversations with people he would always begin by posing a question and then reject any answer as incomplete or incorrect. "We should talk about this more. Ask my secretary to schedule an appointment for you with me for next week." This is how he dismissed ideas suggested to him by his employees.

All his life this man had been scurrying around to establish political relations with "important people." Tirelessly, he would schedule many meetings, make endless phone calls, send hundreds of memos and spend long hours, even weekends, in his office. The position of Principal which he finally succeeded in gaining for himself was, in a sense, the triumph of overbearingness. For his colleagues simply had to give in, either because they were too tired to confront him continuously or because they were loath to be involved in petty discussions. So he succeeded to the throne, but the power which the position implied made him less, not more secure. His anxiety increased and his blood pressure reached dangerous proportions.

It was only after one year of therapy that this life style and behavior was fully revealed and understood for what it was by the patient himself. In the beginning, however, Mr. T. was only asking me questions, basically trying to test my talent and to comment on my expertise, eager to establish a camaraderie between us, the kind of familiarity that later breeds contempt. He came to seek my help but wanted to see me defeated, thereby engaging in the same behavior in my office he suffered from at work. The main goal of the therapy was to bring this man to accept some dependence on me, as his therapist, and on his wife at home. It took him a long time to grasp that a slight change in his role in school, the delegation of some of his responsibilities to others and his dependency on them, do not necessarily detract from his authority. Indeed, a major task of psychotherapy is, as we shall see in the following chapter, to teach patients that there are different ways of playing the roles of a man, a woman, a principal, etc.

Yet, again, it is extremly difficult to bring a patient to renounce his convictions or *names,* mistaken or rigid as they may seem to the observer. And this is not only because his identity is at stake as it expresses itself in these convictions, or that he needs to feel the power and mastery experienced in fitting the world within the boundaries of such *names.* Sometimes it is also because a patient has already established a life style in which he can easily prove that his convictions are right. Like scientists who test and verify their theories in experiments, patients generally manage to verify their beliefs or at least some parts of them in daily experience.

Take for example a person who believes that all his neighbors, if not all people, are selfish creatures who would certainly take advantage of him if they could only find the opportunity. He cites many incidents in which one neighbor did not help him to push his stranded car, another neighbor never bothered to greet him in the street and yet another one even refused to let him borrow his rake. "These and many other incidents," he will say, "only prove how selfish human beings are." Thus, he demonstrates the validity of his conviction by actual events which do not sound far-fetched or implausible. And, furthermore, if one asked the neighbors about this person, it is likely that many would express indifference or even hostility towards him.

But this person might be unaware of the fact that his beliefs tend to act as self-fulfilling prophecies. A belief about the world shapes the behavior of the person holding it. One can easily imagine how a person believing that all people are selfish would behave. He would be guarded, tense and generally stand-offish as he would try to fend off potential threats. "I won't let anyone take advantage of me," he would repeat. He would hardly smile at people, or tell them something about himself, or indulge in those little personal amenities that people exchange to enhance familiarity or friendship. He remains secretive so that no neighbor would "know too much" about him. But then how would people interpret this guardedness, this aloofness? They could easily say that he does not care about them. Some might interpret his aloofness as rejection and resent him. Naturally, people would be generally indifferent to him if not actually rejecting him. And he would immediately seize on their indifference as proof for his original belief that people are selfish. He cannot see that his own behavior makes people shy away from him, that he is himself largely responsible for their attitude toward him and that if he were but to smile at others, they might also smile at him.

Obviously, people strongly encapsulated in *names* cannot always confirm them in actual experience. A moment always comes when even the most zealous belief begins to lose ground because of subtle incongruities between itself and reality. At that moment, a healthy cognition would demonstrate resilience in changing its concepts to accommodate reality whereas a rigid cognition would become defensive instead. A person with rigid beliefs would try to deny the existence of facts contradicting them. "Seeing, they do not see," said Jesus, "and hearing, they do not hear, nor do they understand." All convictions make our perception selective and, therefore, also biased. A person riveted to a single *name* sees reality only in the way he wants to see it and even when confronted with glaring facts belying his ideas, he distorts reality to make it appear concordant with these ideas. The person convinced of the selfishness of all his neighbors would not easily change his mind even if told how some neighbors have given much time and effort for the benefit of the community. "No one does something for nothing," he would grumble, "they are rich and don't have anything else to do anyway."

Again, it is not easy to renounce beliefs, mistaken as they may be. This person may feel lonely and isolated in his neighborhood. He may wish he could love and be loved by people. But this would require from him the admission of being wrong, a change in his basic beliefs and a modification of his behavior towards others. To a rigid person, this might mean losing face, self-esteem, power and self-identity. And he would then fiercely resist this change, become defensive, hostile, paranoid, anxious, panic-stricken, in brief, undergo all the emotional characteristics of a person involved in a protracted struggle for survival. In this struggle he is also likely to become aggressive and hurt other people or destroy whatever stands in the way.

Here we should again touch upon the subject of aggression among people and discuss it in the context of our considerations concerning the insanity of having or not having a *name*. Generally speaking, in the last few decades two camps of scientists have been tackling the problem of aggression, each camp proposing a different point of view. There is on the one hand the camp of ethologists like Lorenz who view aggression as instinctual behavior in man and, on the other hand, there are figures like Skinner and Bandura who dismiss biological explanations of human behavior, including aggression, and instead emphasize that behavior is learned.

According to Lorenz,[1] man possesses a fighting urge that gradually and spontaneously accumulates energy within the body until it is released in one way or another. Lorenz considers this fighting urge more dangerous in man than in other species. The latter have developed, throughout the process of evolution, certain inhibitions to check their aggression so that they would not destroy members of their own species. For example, when dogs aggress against one another, they do so in a relatively harmless way because they have developed rituals to tell one another who is the stronger or who is the vanquished without actually killing one another. Submissive gestures on the part of the vanquished terminate the fight and save the animal from further injury or death. On the other hand, threatening gestures like the dog's growling with exposed teeth, or the monkey's penis erection and open jaws are, often, enough to ward off an enemy, thereby preventing a fight from taking place.

Man, Lorenz claims, is born with the same fighting instincts as lower animals. However, his aggression is poorly checked as he lacks the inhibitions against killing other species have. Also, the development of far-reaching weapons like the sling, the arrow or the gun further decreased the likelihood that such inhibitions would develop. Shooting from afar, man cannot even perceive submissive or other signs that his fellowman might send which could prevent a killing. Consequently, people are bound to kill one another, yielding to their ever-present fighting urge. Lorenz suggests that societies should provide their members with opportunities to discharge their fighting urges, to "drain," so to speak, their aggressive energy in harmless activities so that wars might be avoided. Competitive sports, both national and international, are considered essential in helping people to achieve this goal.

Lorenz' theory has been criticized on many counts, as Montagu shows.[2] Careful studies have shown that not only man kills members of his species; there are many species in which animals kill other members in the fight for females, food or territory. Other studies contested Lorenz' claim that the organism possesses an aggressive instinct and Lorenz was blamed for overlooking in his studies many facts that contradict his basic belief in this instinct. Furthermore, most studies also emphasized the fact that, among animals, killing often depends on environmental factors which might facilitate or prevent its occurrence. Even if one assumes that killing rats is an instinctive urge within the cat, actual killing would depend on learning processes. Kittens raised with rats would generally avoid killing rats whereas kittens raised by a rat-killing mother are very likely to learn the killing of rats.

Theorists like Skinner and Bandura emphasize the role of learning in the development of all human behavior. Bandura[3] states that people might indeed behave aggressively when exposed to adverse treatment but that aggression is by no means the only kind of behavior people resort to in stressful situations. When distressed, some people might show resignation; others seek help and support; others aggress; still others drug themselves with alcohol to forget their troubles and many might try to overcome their difficulties constructively. Bandura emphasizes that aggressive behavior is not an instinctive response in man but rather one response among many which man learns from his fellowmen to cope with difficult situations. It follows, according to this view, that wars among nations or killing among people can in principle be avoided or "unlearned." Aggression is not an ineluctable fate humanity must tolerate forever.

However, we find that neither this approach nor the ethologist's emphasis on the instinctive origin of aggression is a sufficient explanation of aggression in man. It is indeed indisputable that the environment, both physical and human, influences man's behavior and that he generally learns from other people many patterns of conduct. From "bad boys" we indeed learn to swear, kick, etc. Bandura carefully demonstrated that children easily model themselves on others and learn specific ways of showing aggression. Whether to drop an A-bomb, use a sling or simply club someone over the head is something one learns from others. But we should note first that Bandura speaks of aggression only in the negative destructive sense which he considers a learned response to hostile treatment. It was, rather, ethologists like Lorenz, Storr and Eibl-Eibesfeldt who emphasized the positive aspect of aggression as revealed in man's spontaneous drive for life, procreation and other forms of human creativity. Secondly, Skinner, Bandura and the whole camp known as behavior modifiers, as well as the ethologists, have been blind to the dialectical aspect of human cognition which sheds a different light on the problem of aggression.

Human beings are cognitive units constantly interacting with one another, and their interaction is not mechanical and external like the way billiard balls touch one another from the outside. No, human cognitions are interlocked and interrelated to one another in relations of contrast which are analogous to the way figure and background interrelate to form our perception. People have to relate to one another for they draw their personal qualifications from one another. Therefore, human relations at some point always produce aggression. In any perception, when one stimulus becomes the figure, it necessarily relegates all other stimuli to the periphery of the field of vision. Figure and background are in constant interdependency as well as rivalry. By the same token, every time man says "I think" he introduces a new point of view into the world, creates a new identity which forces other points of view, other identities into the background. Since self-identity consists, as we saw, of points of view or cognitive Towers, the birth of any new point of view (positive aggression) is also a threat (negative aggression) against other identities. Since identities are interdependent, aggression among them is unavoidable. We saw a palpable example of this aggression in the history of painting where on the one hand a classic figure overshadows and dwarfs its environment and, on the other hand, a romantic environment engulfs and dissolves the particular figure. This perennial fight in painting between the central figure and the other figures in its environment is only an expression of the basic interrelatedness and rivalry between human identities.

Thus, in human relations, aggression is not confined only to physical damage or killing inflicted on people. We know the vehemence with which societies defend their values and the resistance any new idea encounters until it is accepted. One aggresses against people simply by introducing new beliefs into the world since these beliefs threaten to sweep away traditional values and change their identities. Many would prefer physical death to loss of their identities. Neither the ethologists nor behaviorists like Skinner and Bandura paid attention to issues concerning man's identity nor did they analyze aggression in this context. Yet man is not simply an animal but rather a thinking animal. In creating new ideas or new Towers, he will always aggress against established identities. Rather than asking men to stifle their creativity, societies should help them develop cognitive resilience capable of absorbing and profiting from such creatively aggressive acts.

Now it is obvious that when a person remains locked up in a single role, in a single identity, he is less resilient. The person frozen in one *name* is more likely to resort to negative aggression because his identity is constantly at stake. Rigid in his thoughts, he cannot incorporate other points of view but sees them rather as a direct menace to his existence. So he attacks others as a reaction to his own constant fear. He slanders, vilifies, depreciates the value of other people or, all other ways failing, abuses them physically. In the previous chapter we spoke about the insane person who, not having a *name,* suddenly acquires a new identity which he defends fanatically. Obviously, he will tend to be belligerent or assaultive, desperately defending his newly purchased *name*. On the other hand, a person who is already cast and molded into a rigid identity would be equally fanatic in the face of any novelty in his environment. He would be afraid of losing his mind or his identity were he to introduce the slightest change in his self-identity. Thus, the insanity of not having a *name* and the insanity of having a *name* are interrelated.

The question is, then, how to bring a person to renounce outmoded Towers without making him feel he is losing his mind. How can one develop cognitive resilience in rigid minds? Many people would prefer the comfort of the beaten track or the familiarity of old habits even though these have become useless or, even, fatal. The people of Sodom did not want to renounce their familiar environment and established life style. Lot's wife could not emotionally separate herself from her city. So they all perished. Only Lot could leave Sodom without looking backward. He was resilient enough to accept changes in his identity and therefore survived. However, it was not easy. The Bible says that the angels urged him to leave the city "but he lingered." This leave-taking, this relinquishing of what he had built and loved, demanded enormous strength which he did not possess. So the angels "seized him . . . by the hand, the Lord being merciful to him, and they brought him forth and set him outside the city." The therapist and educator must extend the same helping hand to his patients or students to help them renounce specific *names* or cross the boundaries of rigid identities in which they have imprisoned themselves. But how are they to accomplish this task?

CHAPTER 6

The Babel Therapist

Before treating a patient, the therapist should have a model of a sane mind. Symbolically, we found this model in the half-accomplished, half-destroyed Tower of Babel which denotes sane identity not as a static entity, but rather as a process. We have seen that sane identity always remains elusive, constantly is in the making, an image which is constantly being formed yet never accomplished. The people of Babel sought to acquire a *name,* yet they avoided confining themselves to the finality of a specific one. What this story tells is that sane minds both dread and are drawn to the precarious, the unknown or the ambiguous in life. They yearn for the familiarity and safety of a haven, yet also seek the mysteries of the sea. Caught between these contradictory drives, a healthy or "normal" identity is one that is in flux. It is a dialectical process which alternately strives to crystallize and to rebel against a fixed identity. Psychotherapy should therefore be a training in identity formation and the therapist himself should be a Babel therapist, i.e., an elusive identity both with and without a *name,* a priest with and without a "church." Here the word "church" refers to any theory explaining the causes of mental disturbances as well as recommending measures for their cure.

Today we witness a proliferation of schools of therapy, an overflow of soul healers all seriously striving to help us save our souls. These are: traditional psychoanalysis, behavior modification, group therapy, nude therapy, sensitivity groups, marital counseling, sex therapy, assertive training, etc. Generally speaking, all these approaches aim at a definite goal which the patient is expected to achieve. No matter what the therapeutic philosophy or strategy involved, the therapist seeks to elicit a certain change in his patients. He wants to transfer him from situation A, defined as "abnormal," "intolerable" or "insane," to situation B where the patient supposedly finds himself somehow changed, free from this or that symptom. There is not yet a general agreement among therapists as to what constitutes a pathological symptom and each would also have a different opinion as to what defines mental health. Nevertheless, each sees a specific goal in therapy which he tries to achieve. This goal might be restricted—as is the case in behavior modification—to a simple change in a specific behavior. For example, a therapist would want to suppress thumb-sucking in a four-year-old child. Other therapists might instead aim at helping the patient relieve his anxiety, discharge his pent-up feelings, change his communication pattern or, more pretentiously, change his entire personality. Thus, in each approach there is a specific *something,* a definable milestone or a particular psychic awareness which is considered the goal of the therapy.

The Babel therapist also aims to change behavior or cognitive states. He, too, seeks to help the patient change "intolerable" conditions. Ultimately, however, he does not focus on a specific condition to change or on its specific contents, but rather on the patient's *cognitive resilience* as an abiding condition for any change. In this sense, the Babel therapist is not only goal-oriented but also aimless and vague in his approach. In this he reflects the two antithetical—the classic and romantic—aspects of his patient's search for identity.

To assign only one goal or a single *name* to therapy, whatever this *name* is, would not contribute to the patient's sanity. For example, there is Freud's attempt to interpret human aberrant behavior only on the basis of early childhood experience. He believed he discovered a universal explanation for human neurotic conduct as well as for many of man's dreams, aspirations and failures. He related them to man's emotional and sexual conflicts of early childhood. Anxiety, depression, chronic fatigue and other neurotic symptoms were assumed to be masked expressions of early sexual urges and conflicts when the child wished to possess the parent of the opposite sex, yet feared the punishment that this incest would precipitate. These early sexual desires, although deeply repressed in the unconscious mind of the adult, presumably continue to demand gratification and are therefore at the base of much of the "irrational" behavior of man. Therefore, to relieve a patient of his symptoms, a psychoanalyst believes he should make him aware of this link between his present behavior and the repressed conflicts of the past. And like Isaiah who promised a day when "the wolf shall dwell with the lamb," Freud believed that once we become aware of the unconscious lust of our early childhood, peace will be restored in our minds, and perhaps also upon the earth.

We should hurriedly add that not even Freud could long maintain this certainty in treating man's complex nature. In his later years he sounded more pessimistic about the outcome of psychoanalysis as he realized that not all patients would respond favorably to it.[1] But the idea itself of interpreting the human mind according to one principle, confining human consciousness to a single (sexual) frame of reference resembles the insanity of having a specific *name* which we described earlier. This does not mean that Freud and many other psychoanalysts did not help their patients. In fact, this therapeutic approach might sometimes be more effective than other, more modern methods. But when it is successful, the beneficial effect it has on the patient does not really depend on the theory of infantile sexuality, the repression of that sexuality, and its release by psychoanalysis. As we shall show, in clinical practice many psychoanalysts are unknowingly, and despite themselves, Babel therapists. Their success is due to certain types of ambiguity, vagueness and aimlessness inherent in their styles of communication and not to the Freudian theory itself to which they officially pledge allegiance.

It would be interesting at this point to summarize briefly the history of psychotherapy in this century in order to show that there is more than one approach to treatment, that there is no single one to be employed to the exclusion of the rest.

Like the classic tradition in painting which places the figure in the center of the perceptual field and emphasizes its identity at the expense of the figures pushed into the background, early psychiatry (Kraepelin, Bleuler, Freud) placed the individual person at the focus of its attention, relegating the patient's social environment to a subordinate status. In a typically classic approach, Freud attempted to depict man's "essence" behind his appearances. Sensitive to contradictions and ambiguities in our thoughts, behavior and dreams, Freud attempted to build a unified image of man. In assuming the existence of the unconscious, he could reconcile and harmonize overt inconsistencies in man's appearances, thereby forming a coherent identity awareness in the mind of his patients and followers. Once the unconscious is postulated, patients find it easier to tolerate in themselves contradictory attitudes or incongruous patterns of behavior such as being on the one hand stingy and on the other hand overgenerous, gullible and guarded, optimistic and pessimistic, loving and hating, etc. In an ingenious intellectual hocus-pocus, Freud could simultaneously unite different and opposing human features into one coherent representation of human identity.

It is obvious, however, that any classic representation of identity is but a relative determination. There always remains the question whether any specific representation of this or that object indeed exhausts all its facets or points of view. We recall the struggle of Cubism to depict volume in the figure on the canvas, a task which classic art could not achieve. We also saw that along with this emphasis on the object's volume, objects ceased to be treated —both by Cubists and Futurists— individualistically, as if they were indeed distinct from their environment. On the contrary, figures were made to reflect their relations with other objects as well as with their surrounding space. Now, a similar shift of focus from the individual person to the relations he maintains with his environment was also effected in psychiatry when therapists began to concentrate not only on the individual but also on his human environment or family. In many cases it was found that if therapy indeed improved the patient's feelings and helped him to regard himself anew, his social environment (parents, siblings) tended to resent this change, often even attempting to eradicate it. In one way or another the new "image" or identity of the treated patient clashed with other identities in his social environment. Consequently, to treat the patient and elicit a change in his condition one had to treat the whole family. Family therapy came increasingly to the fore the more investigators learned of the connections between the patient's pathology and the patterns of communication in his home.

Needless to say, this shift of focus from the isolated patient to his family reflected a similar shift in personality theories. Theorists like Mead, Sullivan and Erikson stressed the interpersonal make-up of the individual. Man was no longer considered an independent unit but literally an intersection of various human relations or environmental forces. Thus, in opting to treat the entire family, therapists acquired a wider identity awareness of man as compared with the Freudian one. In viewing the patient's mental disturbance as a reflection of the familial sickness, and in attempting to change the entire family system, therapists also make their patients acquire this wide awareness of themselves. These patients are told, for example, that they are social products modeled after the roles of the father and the mother, the man and the woman which their parents played at home. They are shown how their environment acts on them and how they can, in return, react and change it. The nature, the cause, as well as the objective of the treatment are explained to them in interpersonal terms.

In various trends of the community mental health movement that has recently developed, the patient's pathology is being considered in the light of even wider environmental factors such as the neighborhood in which the patient grew up, his peer group, his social class, etc.[2] From this point of view, treating a patient does not mean to look for a "disease" inside him as is the case in the traditional medical model of psychiatry, but rather to understand and treat his symptom in the total environmental context in which it developed. For example, the disruptive behavior and academic underachievement of a black boy at school will induce the environmentally oriented therapist to look for the links between this behavior and the boy's environment at home as well as at school. Obviously, in studying the atmosphere of the boy's home, or in delineating a course of treatment, the therapist must be familiar with the nature and idiosyncrasies of the Black culture as opposed to the Jewish or Italian culture. What this means is that unlike a psychoanalyst who approaches the patient with a universal therapeutic model that can presumably explain and treat pathology in all persons, the environmentally oriented therapist understands and treats problematic behavior more from the individual patient's, rather than from his own, point of view.

To take another example, if a certain culture encourages dependency of women on men, and if a therapist happens to treat a depressed woman coming from this background, any attempt to change her state would take into consideration the woman's background. Therefore, instead of trying to change her value system and make her an entirely independent person, the therapist would try to reorganize her dependency relations with her husband or parents in a more satisfactory way from *her* point of view. In this approach, the therapist does not possess universal labels that would apply to and restructure the cognition of all patients. Essentially, every patient becomes a new puzzle for the therapist to solve. He lays before the therapist only pieces of his self-image, bits of his past history and fragmented descriptions of his environment. The therapist's task is not only to arrange these pieces so that he can clearly identify the patient's condition, but also to determine the best configuration in which several factors in the patient's life could be rearranged so that the patient can resolve his psychological problems. Success in therapy would then depend on the scope of the therapist's awareness of his patient's identity and on the extent to which this cognitive identity reflects the patient's complex relations with his cultural milieu.

But the more one emphasizes the patient's relations with his environment, the more one runs the risk of losing sight of the patient's total picture. We saw that in some Futurist and romantic paintings, an overemphasis on the object's relations with its surroundings fragments or atomizes the object itself to the extent that the painting appears without a focus. The object dissolves into its environment, thereby losing its specific identity. Some romantic paintings (Kandinsky's, for example) are not even meant to represent any object's identity; they are only expected to evoke feelings or moods in the beholder. By the same token, psychological theories showing exaggerated interest in the patient's environment or in his specific acts within this environment might blur the image of the person's identity. It is like losing sight of the forest when one concentrates on the individual trees.

Thus, the proponents of behavioral therapy generally focus not on the totality of the person, but on his specific symptoms: the fear of dogs, anxiety aroused in elevators or disruptive behavior at school. In each case a specific response in a specific environment is being studied and treated. Total identity awareness of man expressed in general concepts like the "ego" or the "self" are ignored or flatly rejected as being mere abstractions. Although some behavioral theorists, like Mischel,[3] also stressed the unity or the consistency in human behavior, most behavioral theories do not offer a holistic conception of man but rather depict him as being atomized into a multiplicity of behavioral responses. The emphasis is laid on this or that environmental stimulus to account for this or that particular symptom or behavior. There is no interest in the person as a whole.

In other contemporary schools of therapy—for example, the "encounter group" and "sensitivity group" movements—man's relations to his environment, especially to other people, are even more pronounced than in behavioral therapies although, unlike the latter, they are expressed in emotional terms. Consequently, similar to some romantic paintings, these trends do not particularly aim at forming any object identity in the patient's mind but rather seek to evoke moods in him. Therapists of these movements commonly describe their goals as being the development of sensitivity in the person, the discharge of feelings, learning to feel, the enhancement of awareness, etc. This is done within a group setting where group members are encouraged to interact with one another and openly express their feelings. But in many such groups, the collective emotional excitement leaves little privacy to the individual member. In the name of honesty and openness, these groups often encroach upon the ego boundaries of the individual member who gradually loses his distinctive identity while identifying with the group. Significantly, some encounter groups have turned into nude groups. Clothes, symbols of privacy and expressions of individual differences among people, are abolished to further accentuate relatedness and openness among group members. But the question is whether any member can maintain his individuality in this romantic overemphasis on relatedness. And the answer is often in the negative.

In itself, this development in psychotherapy, from the classic Freudian approach to the romantic "sensitivity group" trend, only demonstrates the elusiveness of man's identity as well as the difficulty in establishing causes or treatment of mental disturbances.

On the one hand, a clear-cut picture of man is given and the causes of his symptoms as well as their cure appear well-defined. On the other hand, there is no interest in portraying a whole and distinct picture of man or in reducing his psychological malaise to specific causes in his past or in his environment. Therapy concentrates instead on man's feelings and moods, vague and incoherent as they might appear.

Thus, as the history of therapy indicates, there is no universal cure for mental distress and it would be completely misleading to wear the gown of the scientist and claim that such a cure indeed exists. Every therapeutic approach has claimed success with many patients who might indeed say that they felt cured after the treatment they received. However, the fact that a patient starts to feel better is not necessarily a direct result of the treatment but rather an outcome of a cognitive change within the patient. For example, a therapist might recommend "emotional discharge," "primal scream" or awareness of early sexual conflicts as *the* magical cure for mental troubles. But then when mental relief is indeed felt, it does not result from the "primal scream" or the emotional discharge itself but rather from cognitive elements which all therapeutic approaches share. No matter what therapeutic method one employs, it involves an encounter and communication between two cognitions, the patient's and the therapist's. Since all patients suffer from the insanity of having and the insanity of not having a *name*, a therapist would help a patient by providing him with a *name* as well as making him renounce a stultified one. And this is what the Babel therapist does; he is a priest with and without a "church."

We will now progressively see that regardless of their affiliation to this or that form of therapy, therapists are successful to the extent they adopt the cognitive approach of the Babel therapist.

Priesthood with a "Church"

Is the bottle half-empty or half-full? The answer to this question has traditionally distinguished the pessimist from the optimist. Our moods do not depend only on the material things we see but also on the way we interpret them. Two people can see the same data about, for example, the financial condition of the country. One might interpret them in a way to show that there is a great hope for improvement and would therefore turn many listeners as well as himself into optimists. The other person might see the same data as early signs of national bankruptcy and plunge himself and others into despair. The nature of our emotions or moods depends then on the labels we attach to reality or to the "church" to which we adhere.

For years scientists have been unsuccessfully trying to define emotions or to differentiate between them according to the physiological changes that take place in the body when one experiences an emotion. In this way, bodily responses like shaking, running, nail biting, heart palpitation, sweating, the flow of adrenalin into the blood stream, hand temperature, etc., were each considered to indicate an emotional state. However, it became evident that different emotions—for example, joy and anger—could have similar bodily manifestations in a certain person; his pulse rate would be the same or he would perspire to the same degree. It was then realized that cognitive labels, not simply physiological changes in the body, would determine whether we are happy or sad, pessimistic or optimistic.

In one study, Schachter and Singer injected adrenalin into subjects participating in their experiment and manipulated the situation in such a way as to prove that cognitive labels, not only the presence of adrenalin in the blood, will determine what emotion one will feel.[4] After the drug was injected, the subjects were divided into different groups in which the experimenters "planted" trained companions who presumably received the same injection. In one group, the "planted" subject was instructed to act euphorically, that is, to be playful and gay, doodling, making paper airplanes, playing "basketball" by throwing wads of paper into the wastebasket and encouraging other members in his experimental group to do the same. In another group, the "planted" subject was instead instructed to play at being angry, that is, to complain about the experiment, resent the questionnaire which he and his partners had to fill out, etc. Now, there were many aspects to this experiment, but what interests us most is the fact that those subjects who did not know the nature of adrenalin, that is, did not expect to be "emotional" in one way or another, were markedly influenced by the cognitive labels provided to them through the "planted" subjects. Those who observed the "euphoric" subject became euphoric, and those who observed the "angry" one became angry.

In another experiment, Valins asked his subjects to rate their preference for slides of semi-nude girls while listening to sounds that were allegedly their heart beats.[5] Most of us would expect that heart rates in men would increase in response to photographs of nude women. In this experiment it was expected that the thought "That girl has affected my heart rate" would induce the subjects to consider the girl more attractive. The participating subjects were led to believe that the heart beat they heard through the earphones was their own whereas in reality it was not. For half the slides they saw, the experimenter deliberately changed the heart rate, thereby cognitively suggesting to the subjects that they were "more excited." Consequently, the subjects preferred these slides to the others which were not allied to the false heart beat. Even after four or five weeks, the subjects continued to believe that the former girls were more attractive. Beauty, as has been said, does not lie in the object but rather in the eyes of the beholder. In this experiment, beauty was determined, so to speak, by the ears not the eyes of the beholder. The subjects based their judgment on the false feedback of their heartbeats.

Whether a scene is frightening, revolting, interesting or boring would depend, as Lazarus amply demonstrated, on the *cognitive appraisals* of the person viewing the scene.[6] It is *names* that determine what we feel or whether feelings are sane or insane. Here, Davison's treatment of a schizophrenic patient by "cognitive structuring" is noteworthy.[7] The patient complained about twitches over his eyes, heart and solar plexus. Particularly annoying to him were the "pressure points" which he felt over his right eye. He believed that they were caused by a "spirit" that was helping him to make decisions. However, the patient's condition worsened as he felt he was confused by conflicting "messages." He became increasingly worried and when he was hospitalized, he was overtly delusional, fearing persecution from others and expressing other incoherent ideas that somehow related to information coming from his "pressure points."

The "cognitive structuring" or treatment of this patient consisted essentially in offering him different, "normal" *names* for his feelings. He was told that the pressure points were actually physical indications of tension and stress coming from his environment, not from a "spirit." He was also shown how muscle relaxation might help relieve this pressure. The patient gradually stopped referring to "spirit-induced sensations" but merely to "sensations." Sanity was thereby established by attributing what he felt to environmental and physiological rather than to magical or mythical factors.

Needless to say, in other societies this patient's sanity could have been restored differently, for example, by placating or exorcising the "spirit" in him. Every society has its own "church" to distinguish right from wrong, God from the Devil and the sane from the insane. It is a social consensus that determines what sanity is or what belief would be the cure for this or that illness. As Frank amply demonstrated, it is *persuasion,* namely cognitive belief that cures many illnesses, not only mental but sometimes also physical.[8] The shaman's words, the utterances of dervishes or the prayers of priests have saved many souls as they fill the patients with hopes, bolster their self-esteem and strengthen their ties with their community. In modern medicine, too, the cognitive power of placebos has long been recognized. Cognitive suggestions can turn any neutral substance or water into a magical drug.

No matter what therapeutic method one employs, or what "church" one belongs to, all tend to cause cognitive changes in the patients. In the final analysis, it appears that all therapies help the patients by giving *names* to their troubled conditions, thereby changing their views about the world. Even when a therapist in a "sensitivity training" group seeks to evoke only feelings in his patients, he indirectly communicates to them cognitive labels concerning what is "good" or "bad," sane or insane in their behavior. In this case, sanity would be linked to the ability to feel and mental troubles to emotional constriction. Psycho-analysis, on the other hand, explicitly sets cognitive awareness of unconscious conflicts as the main goal of therapy. Behavioral therapy also achieves its goal through cognitive changes in the patient's mind, this despite Skinner's or Wolpe's resistance to recognizing the existence of cognitive factors in their procedures.

Behavior modification as a method of treatment developed in direct opposition to the traditional, "insight oriented" therapy. Whereas for Freud symptoms like anxiety, depression, chronic fatigue, phobias, etc., are manifestations of unconscious conflicts, for Wolpe they are merely learned responses that can be unlearned or extinguished through desensitization procedures. To take an example, Wolpe or another behavior modifier would not consider a phobia about horses an indi-cation of hidden sexual conflicts in the patient but rather a learned response. It is most probable that the patient had been frightened by a horse at one point in his past and since that time this fear has spread to all horses and become an incapacitating phobia. Wolpe would there-fore have the patient in his office, ask him to relax and, while relaxing, imagine a horse approaching him. For instance, the patient would first imagine the horse as being hundred yards away, then seventy-five yards, then fifty, and so on until the patient could touch the horse in his imagination. If at any point, say at the fifty yard distance, the patient would start to feel anxious, Wolpe would ask him to relax and then again imagine the horse at seventy-five yards, seventy yards and so forth. Thus, just as we inoculate a patient with weaker bacteria so that he develops resistance to a disease, Wolpe would present an imaginary horse to the patient. This, coupled with the relaxed condition of the patient would eventually inhibit the patient's anxiety or desen-sitize it.

This mode of therapy has indeed proven to be very effective but its effectiveness is now attributed to many cognitive factors which Wolpe overlooked.[9] Wolpe liked to explain the process of desensiti-zation while drawing on Pavlov's and Hull's learning theories which concentrated on learning processes manifested both by animals and human beings. But human beings have cognitive abilities that animals apparently lack and which certainly contribute to any process of desen-sitization. There is first the patient's ability to imagine, for example a horse, a dog or whatever the phobia-arousing object is. Secondly, there is the ability to introspect and attend to inner feelings and then report them to the therapist. Furthermore, there are the patient's expectations to feel better, to be cured, the intense belief that the doctor can create miracles, the urge to be a "good" patient who should not fail the doctor, etc. All these factors determine the outcome of behavioral therapy just as they enhance the effectiveness of shamans and dervishes. And the outcome itself in behavioral therapy is basically cognitive, not only behavioral. Before the treatment, the horse was *fearful* or *monstrous* in the patient's eyes. After the treatment the horse came to be regarded as *harmless* or even *great*.

Whether through feedback techniques, Transcendental Meditation, Yoga or relaxation techniques, patients learn to reduce their blood pressure, control their pulse or body temperature, overcome migraine headache or other pains. But behind these methods there always lies the power of cognitive suggestions, the charm of words which, as Gorgias the Sophist said, sooth and relieve, gladden and shape the soul.[10] When in distress, panic or bewilderment, patients expect the therapist to give them *names,* for their distress originated from the lack of a *name.* So, they ask about the cause of their symptoms, the name of their trouble and the way to treat it. They ask for advice or guidance. How to handle a marital conflict? What to do with one's life? Marry or not marry? How to deal with the spouse's continued dependency on her parents? Is it "good" or "bad" to pamper children? In brief, the therapist must define the patient's condition for the patient as well as advise him what would be the wisest thing to do in this or that situation. For only in analyzing the patient's predicament and advising him to change his life in this or that way can the latter extricate himself from his troubled situation.

But here we are touching upon a highly sensitive issue intimately related to the value system of our society. Should a therapist tell a patient what to do? Aren't we all free individuals in a free society? Don't we all admire the image of independent John Wayne? Would we dare tell John Wayne what to do? Besides, there is also the moral issue involving the abuse of the therapist's authority in exploiting the patient in one way or another. Important as these questions are, they have been answered, unfortunately, evasively or hypocritically by many therapists.

For Freud and the psychoanalysts, this issue has not aroused much concern for they have considered themselves objective scientists whose task is to help the patient discover in himself a mental abscess, so to speak, making him aware of his unconscious libidinal conflicts of early childhood, which are presumably at the root of all his troubles. So, the analyst is supposedly only a catalyzer who patiently and impartially listens to the patient's words, associations, dreams, etc., gently guiding him in such a way that the patient gains insight as to the connection between his symptoms and his unconscious wishes. Obviously, according to this philosophy, the therapist remains ethically "clean." He cannot possibly mislead the patient as he never tells him what to do or what to say. Analysts are also trained to be aware of countertransference processes in which they might read their own emotional lives in their patients'.

However, the very assumption that the unconscious exists, that our adult neurotic behavior presumably reflects oral, anal or phallic conflicts of early childhood is a definitive form of cognitive structuring. To tell a person that he has an unconscious mind is, in principle, not different from other beliefs in other societies where mental distress is attributed to spirits and fiends. This is not to detract from the effectiveness of psychoanalysis which, as we shall soon explain, might be extremely helpful in many cases. But it would be misleading to claim that the psychoanalyst is indeed an impartial judge. For psychoanalysis passes general judgments on patients even before seeing them. It is determined that human troubles *must* in one may or another reflect early libidinal conflicts and woe to the patient if he denies it! For then he would be considered "resisting," "denying" or "persisting" in his neurotic patterns to mask unconscious themes. Thus, far from being an impartial catalyzer, the psychoanalyst actively forms the patient's cognition with a specific *name* which would help him reconcile many contradictory and "irrational" aspects of his personality. This is a direct cognitive structuring.

The Rogerian therapeutic approach is even keener than psychoanalysis in emphasizing the non-directing, non-structuring role of the therapist. Rogerians generally loathe behavioral treatments which seek to reinforce or extinguish this or that behavior in people. Such a behavioral approach would appear to them dehumanizing and mechanistic, beneath the dignity of man. For man's behavior should not be controlled in any way, because man is considered a free agent capable of making his own decisions, and any structuring technique employed by the therapist would only harm the patient's free spirit. What is, then, the role of the therapist? He is supposed to be a warm, fatherly figure who offers his unconditional attention to his patient. It is assumed that this approach will help the patient discover in himself many potentialities, new sources of energy and existential possibilities which he will then, with the support of the therapist, bring to realization. There is a marked flavor of romanticism in Rogers' theory, placing high value on the constant development of personality and decrying its encapsulation in any single form of existence.

However, despite such protestations, a strictly non-structuring or noncommittal therapy does not exist. Like all men, patients look for cognitive Towers to organize their world and when they come to therapy, they expect to receive an interpretation of their symptoms as well as learn their causes. Failure to offer them this cognitive interpretation or structuring would only leave them more anxious and bewildered than they were. It would be misleading to claim that a therapist is an impartial judge. All therapists influence their patients. It has been shown that the Rogerian, presumably non-directing therapists nevertheless control their patients' behaviors by their silence, smiles or other nonverbal communication.[11] For an interested look on the face of the therapist or a benevolent smile could suffice to convey to a crying patient that crying is a "good" response that should not be avoided. On the other hand, the therapist's silence could be considered disapproval, and *is,* often enough to make the patient avoid behaving in a certain way. Also, the therapist's image or the décor of his office could indirectly tell the patient how a "successful person" should look and behave. After all, the therapist is viewed as an authority figure by his patient and every gesture he makes is likely to be interpreted as meaningful in one way or another and thereby becomes an influential element in the therapy.

On the other hand, behavioral therapy is straightforwardly directive. Here there is no attempt to mask the influence of the therapist on his patient, for the therapist usually looks for factors in the patient's environment which would reinforce or suppress certain behavior in the patient. This environment can also be the therapist's office where the therapist exercises his authority and uses his charm (if he has it) to motivate the patient to change something in his behavior that would eventually make him feel better. Or the therapist might give specific instructions to a teacher or to a parent, teaching him how to control the acting-out behavior in a young child.

Thus, whether directly or indirectly, willfully or accidentally, every effective therapist comes to represent a "church" in the eyes of his patients. He always gives them clues or *names* as to the origins of their troubles, or what they should do in order to improve. Therapy always involves processes of identity formation in which the nature of the symptom's cause or its antidote is established. One therapist would attribute mental disturbances to the influence of "spirits," another therapist would point to the "unconscious" and yet another would establish a "rational" cause. What is important to notice is that the symptoms are always attributed to a "something," an identity in which the therapist believes.[12]

And we cannot say that this "something" or identity that explains or cures mental illness is an "objective" fact, independent of the therapist's subjective impression. Even when organic disturbances are clearly the major cause of a mental disease, tranquilizers and other medications would not solve the patient's perplexities or the problems he might have with his parents, wife or colleagues. The latter would be treated by the therapist's appraisal and structuring that would determine what is real or unreal, sane or insane in the patient's mind. But this structuring itself depends on the cognitive Towers of the society in which the therapist lives. Societies that believe in spirits would also effectively cure mental illness with their help. A therapist can use any *name* or identity in order to explain and cure mental disturbances provided, however, that he fits his explanations into the cognitive system of the society in which he functions so that the patient could test and validate these explanations outside the therapist's office. Sometimes, therapists are compared to witch doctors, especially when their suggestive power is being recognized. It is to be noted, however, that in primitive societies, the position of a witch doctor is difficult to attain for it requires high intelligence and many years of training to be fully familiar with society's cognitive system and cultural heritage. No suggestive power is effective unless the therapist accommodates his approach to the cognitive system of his patient. Thus, the "something" that the therapist offers as an explanation or a treatment for mental disturbances, is not a totally "subjective" or arbitrary identity. Obviously, therapy will not be successful if the therapist attempts to restructure the patient's bewildered mind with socially unacceptable cognitions.

Thus, as a priest with a "church," the therapist sees as his goal the cognitive restructuring of the patient's mind. Either because of a situational crisis, a biological disturbance or both, the patient's state of mind as well as his behavior deviate from socially accepted norms. Since mental difficulties almost always relate to concrete life situations, the therapist will have to answer the patient's questions about the right way to behave or the right action to take. Ultimately, then, the therapist's task consists in helping the patient accommodate himself to the social system in which he lives. In this way, the therapist reinstates the patient's self-identity and gives his existence meaning in having him readjust to his social environment. Emotionally, the goal of this therapy is to reduce the patient's fears and anxieties which had originated in his unstructured condition. On the other hand, it also arouses hopes and expectations in the patient's mind as to his abilities to function again, forgetting his recent failures and regaining the sense of achievement.

But the question remains: Could the therapist mislead his patient? Given that all therapists influence their patients, it is indeed possible that the latter can be misdirected, brainwashed and exploited in one way or another. By providing cognitive structuring, therapists can induce blind conformity in their patients, enslave them to rigid forms of existence and stifle their vitality. Indeed, a patient suffering from the insanity of not having a *name,* from the bewilderment and passivity of meaningless existence, will be eager to receive a *name* from his therapist. But, by providing him with structuring, the therapist might induce in him the other kind of insanity, namely, the insanity of having a *name.*

And the possibility of misleading a patient is not restricted to immoral therapists. For, as has been said, the way to perdition is strewn with good intentions. Uncertainties are still inherent in the psychological lore, and psychotherapy has not yet reached the level of an exact science. It therefore cannot provide *absolutely* adequate and valid *names* to patients. Skinner harbors the pretension of having turned psychology into an exact science capable of accurately measuring and controlling human behavior. But this can be done only if one ignores the cognitive aspect of human behavior or the fact that man is not simply an animal but rather a thinking animal. In itself, Skinner's learning theory is simple and understandable: We learn a behavior that has been reinforced or that "pays off" and avoid others which do not. It is also easy to prove the soundness of this principle in laboratories while dealing with animals. Give a banana to a monkey each time it screams and it will soon learn to be insistent, even vociferous in its demands (assertive therapy). Give it a candy each time it exposes its teeth and it will soon adopt the "keep smiling" philosophy. By the same token we can assume that our life style, habits and attitudes were gradually learned and shaped by rewards and punishments visited upon us by our parents, grandparents or society in general.

But while the principle of learning is simple to understand, it is not easy to determine, especially when dealing with human beings, what precisely makes them acquire this or that behavior. What would reinforce a human being and make him happy? A banana? A glass of beer? Is a reinforcement something that would make him excited or is it rather a pacifier of some kind?* We saw that the organism enjoys a reduction of bodily tension, a mild increase of tension as well as a combination of both. Most reinforcements shaping behavior of people are complex in nature, and their complexity stems from the fact that man is a thinking animal. Skinner and his followers have ignored the thinking part of man, the classic as well as the romantic tendencies of his mind, his constant striving for the known as well as the unknown, for the real as well as the mythological. Ignoring the elusiveness of man's nature, it was easy to equate his behavior to the behavior of rats and monkeys studied in laboratories and to believe that one can predict and control his conduct with scientific accuracy.

Thus, when trying to treat a patient, the therapist has to consider the right mixture of pacifying and exciting, socially gratifying and arousing factors that would improve his condition. And conjectures do not constitute exact science. They can be erroneous and misleading, especially when the therapist is unfamiliar with the patient's cultural background which generally determines what would be reinforcing for the latter. Nevertheless, the therapist has to take the risk and provide his patient with a *name,* an explanation for his condition and a way out. We saw that reality is not a given phenomenon but

---

* In fact, the definition of reinforcement is neutral as to specifications of content. As defined by Premack,[13] reinforcement is a relative property expressed by the probability of a response to occur. For any pair of responses, the one that has a higher probability of occurrence will reinforce a preceding one with a lower frequency of occurrence. Thus, the definition does not say whether a reinforcement is something that gratifies or arouses or both.

rather a construction of cognitive Towers. The sense of reality is therefore a social product. It is from others that we initially learn *names* constituting this world and patients expect to receive *names* from their therapists. No therapist can avoid this task of cognitive structuring and remain helpful to his patient.

However, giving a *name* to a patient is only one aspect of a therapy that features cognitive resilience. The therapist should not only provide cognitive structuring to his patient but also teach him to renounce fixed *names* and be open to new existential possibilities. And this is what the Babel therapist does, for he is himself a priest with and without a "church."

Priesthood without a "church"

Two tasks await the therapist in his interaction with his patient. He has to restructure the patient's cognitive condition but, in order to achieve this goal, he must also deal with those patient's convictions that stand in the way. No matter how anxious, confused and disturbed a patient may be, he always retains certain opinions about himself or about the world, convictions as to why and how or where his troubles began. A psychotic patient might, in an agitated mood, nevertheless adamantly insist, for example, that ghosts visit him every night to upset his mood. Other patients would attribute their predicaments to "fate," "bad luck," their wives or their neighbors. Although coming to ask for help, advice and guidance, patients also tend to cling to their cognitive systems or parts of these, no matter how shaken or shattered these systems are. We said earlier that patients often swing from a state of not having a *name* to a fanatic belief in this or that *name.* Obviously, the therapist cannot restructure the cognitive state of a patient unless he makes him renounce his adamant, yet mistaken convictions. The patient must practice some accommodation before any change in his condition can take place. Ultimately, the patient would learn to practice this accommodation if he saw his therapist doing the same. To treat the insanity of having a rigid *name,* the therapist must himself appear flexible and amenable. With the earnestness of a priest or of a Socrates, he should admit his ignorance. Thus, while on the one hand he appears strong, "professional" and a believer in a particular "church," on the other hand he acknowledges the relative value of all "churches," their limits and flaws. In this sense he is a priest without a definite "church."

We should recall that the opinions one holds, his beliefs and convictions are the manifestations or expressions of his self-identity. Man's identity consists only in the *names* he gives to other persons or to the world. In developing a conviction or a point of view, man also exercises his creative power as well as his control over his world. For it is with *names* that he organizes and gives meaning to his world which would otherwise lack sense and structure. No wonder then, that most people, not only patients, are generally reluctant to renounce their beliefs for this would entail losing their self-identities or the very meaning of their existence.

Take, for example, a depressed person with a markedly low self-esteem who loathes himself and thinks of suicide. This particular person is convinced that he is a weak and miserable creature, unworthy of love. He also profoundly dislikes the world around him, finding nothing in it for which life is worth living. How could one change this person's gloomy view of himself and his world? Commonly, people who want to help a depressed person will try to console and comfort him while showing signs of concern, care and love. They ask the person to share with them his troubles and would then try to prove to him that, after all, things are not as bad as he thinks, that there is still hope and that he should not despair. Depending on the intensity of their depression, some depressed patients would respond positively to this aproach. They would feel better once they are proven wrong in their harsh self-criticism and in their gloomy beliefs. However, deeply depressed and suicidal patients are less likely to be helped by this approach. They might become even more depressed because of it.

Contradictory through it may seem, underneath the heaviest depression in a patient one can always detect the pride he takes in having a conviction or a determined point of view. Dark and self-deprecating though they are, his views constitute the only concrete mark he has of selfhood or self-identity. Therefore, telling him: "No, you shouldn't be so hard on yourself! You are not a miserable but rather a nice person and I like you very much!" would be a flat rejection of his conviction, a demand that he should renounce the only expression he now has of self-identity. He might choose to commit suicide and take his convictions with him to the grave rather than renounce his identity while being alive. Not only he would mistrust the therapist's words but he would also see in them rejection, which further "proves" how his therapist and the entire world dislike him. After all, to tell him that he is a "nice person" is to dismiss his own evaluation of himself. How could he believe that a therapist who disregards his feelings and convictions nevertheless likes him? Therefore, instead of pulling him out of his depression, this remark would make him sink deeper into it as he realizes how little people understand him.

Or take the paranoid patient. He might believe that his family is trying to "get" him, that they all want him to die in order to inherit his money. He would therefore be continuously suspicious that the food he is being served is poisoned, that the family has hired "agents" to kill him or that some nurses in the hospital have already been paid to strangle him during his sleep. How can one change this patient's mind? To reject his contentions, to tell him flatly that his fears are imaginary would only increase his suspicions. The patient would then place the therapist, too, on the "enemy side" and believe that he is conniving with the family to "get" him. It is counterproductive to dismiss whatever conviction a patient or any person might have if his identity is at stake. Very often the truth is painful to hear and throwing it in a person's face could be an extremely aggressive act, especially when his convictions are expressions of his identity. The patient's or any person's convictions cannot be replaced unless the patient first becomes somewhat puzzled or uncertain about his beliefs. But how does one lead a person to doubt and then to renounce his convictions?

We all entertain some unimportant thoughts and opinions which lie on the periphery of our cognition, which relate to worldly matters, which we regard as marginal or insignificant. Unlike religious beliefs, and ethical or political ideals which might be expressions of self-identity, these unimportant thoughts are easy to change. Renouncing them would leave us unperturbed for they are only free-floating notions about things in relation to which we can afford being gullible, silly or wrong. To put it simply, it would be possible to make a patient renounce certain convictions if one could relegate them to the periphery of the patient's cognition. In other words, the therapist should try to turn the patient's classically focused cognition, which stubbornly centers on a particular conviction, into a more "fluid" or romantic cognition where the same cognition would free-float on the periphery of consciousness together with other cognitions or possibilities. Thus, the insanity of having a *name* is to be treated by introducing more of the romantic aspect into consciousness, thereby neutralizing to some extent the existing fixity of the classical aspect. And it is ambiguity that fulfils this role.

We recall that the Tower of Babel was not destroyed by direct physical force. God only confused the language of its builders so "that they may not understand one another's speech." We also noted that God's action was not a totally destructive act, but rather a disruption which eventually brought about a new variety of languages and nations. We can rightly assume that the confusion in question created factions among the people so that each group developed a different opinion as to how the Tower should be completed. Just as the confusion that God inflicted on the people of Babel could be construed as an ambiguity which created differences that dissolved their unity, so, by the same token, ambiguous communications are the means a therapist uses to make patients renounce their cognitive Towers or convictions. It is not the presentation of a counter-argument or counter-conviction that would soften the patient's rigidity but rather the impact of a cognitive confusion which should result in an awareness of a variety of convictions or possibilities.

Obviously, the problem facing the therapist is how to instill into the patient's mind precise degrees of ambiguity to obtain beneficial results, enriching the mind with the awareness of new possibilities and not bringing it instead to a state of utter confusion. We have already discussed the shattering effect that ambiguity may have on the mind, the relation between double bind—or ambiguous communication—and the development of schizophrenic disturbances. Indeed both results, cognitive richness or total confusion, are likely to obtain depending on the degree of ambiguity communicated. What, then, would be a beneficial ambiguity?

The charm and attraction of many artistic creations lie in the ambiguity they convey. When art is only representational or descriptive it eventually loses its attractiveness and becomes boring. What would distinguish a painting from a photograph or a novel from a mere account of events is the degree of artistic ambiguity they portray. Leonardo's *Mona Lisa* was not meant to be a mere representation or a picture of a woman. For together with the representational elements, the painting also carries an ambiguous message that has continued to puzzle beholders for four centuries. Why does Mona Lisa smile? For a short moment, this enigmatic smile and inscrutable look seem to diffuse feminine warmth, softness and placidity. But then another expression blends into this initial appearance. This time, the look seems aloof, cold, calculating and rejecting. Do the measured smile, the thin lips and the pointed chin betray intransigence or cruelty? Another glance and the woman seems to answer: No, I only meant to tease you and play the rebuking mother. Thus, a multiplicity of facial expressions hinting at different human characteristics start to parade themselves in our imagination almost simultaneously. And one then realizes that Mona Lisa or any other human being might indeed be a combination of different as well as opposing characteristics quite in contrast to our ordinary vision of man which tends to reduce his identity to one or two *names*. In the face of ambiguity, we find ourselves resigned to the idea of multiplicity.

Take another form of artistic ambiguity, this time the character of Macbeth. In his play, Shakespeare did not provide a well-defined identity for his protagonist but rather a congeries of antithetical characteristics that make the spectator ponder human nature deeply. For one cannot sum up Macbeth with a single label. He is a weak and gullible person, easily influenced by his wife to commit a cowardly murder, yet he is also a self-determined warrior who would unflinchingly die for a cause. While preparing himself for the crucial battle, he hears about the death of his wife and he murmurs: " . . . (Life) is a tale told by an idiot full of sound and fury, signifying nothing." But this conviction does not weaken his courage or make him despair. No, he goes to the battle and fights it to the bitter end. Inside him hope and despair somehow cease to be at odds and nourish one another instead. Macbeth, a truly ambiguous figure, forces us to notice new possibilities of human behavior, thereby widening our awareness of the identity of man. Art, as Heidegger puts it, permits reality to unfold itself or lets its multiple facets be.[14] Confronted with these artistic ambiguities, we relax our rigid attitudes, readily reconsider old convictions and open ourselves to new ones.

Most common is the ambiguity to be found in the daily communication between people. For man, as we have said, is a creature capable of communicating two messages at once, which may either confirm or contradict one another. He might speak in the affirmative and support his verbal statement with the nodding of his head or, on the other hand, he might say "yes" while shaking his head to mean "no." This kind of ambiguity is commonly found in ironic or humorous communication that tends to attract as well as baffle unsuspecting listeners. Note the effect of the following example of irony.

It often happens that a person given to irony will state explicitly that which he denies implicitly. For instance, in speaking about Mr. Y. he might say: "You are right, Mr. Y. is a wise man. Yes indeed, Mr. Y. is a *very, very, very* wise man!" The ironist does not say that Mr. Y. is not wise. On the contrary, he affirms Mr. Y's wisdom but does it in a way that suggests its denial. In the face of the "very, very, very wise," Mr. Y's wisdom appears very pale indeed. In this way, an ironic statement makes the listener consider that there exist many degrees of wisdom, that in the case of Mr. Y. he may have been mistaken in attributing to him any wisdom at all. The ironist or the humorist induces us to find qualitative differences in the world, thereby widening our identity awareness. The ambiguity of "yes" and "no" inherent in irony and humor frees consciousness from the confines of one or two narrow facets of reality. In the above, the listener is reminded that wisdom has many degrees and that the world is highly complex.

Kierkegaard was especially interested in this ambiguous mode of communication which he called "indirect communication."[15] He felt that no direct criticism or attack can bring an opponent to renounce his convictions, mistaken as they may be. He therefore recommended this subtle form of communication to teachers and ministers who seek to widen the minds of their fellowmen and free them from the constraints of rigid beliefs. And Kierkegaard pointed to Socrates as the originator of this mode of communication from whom he himself learned it.[16] Socrates used irony constantly in order to free the youths of Athens from their preconceived ideas and prejudices, compelling them to redefine their values.

But ambiguity is part of nature as well as a human product. It is not only couched in man's different forms of communication but is introduced into the world daily by the mystifying contrast of light and darkness at twilight or at dawn. In the dawn's haze or in the moonlight, objects in nature lose their firm contours and shed their familiar identities. A tree in the park starts to look like a giant, human shadows are aggrandized or distorted and most objects are enveloped in uncanny and puzzling layers of the unknown in nature. By definition, the ambiguous is not ordinary but extraordinary. It disrupts the smooth and familiar flow of phenomena that one habitually encounters in routine activities and attracts attention by virtue of this very disruption. Naturally, one can get used to ambiguities and stop paying them attention. A person walking every night through a park is likely to cease reacting to the ambiguities surrounding the objects in the dark. Although human existence is replete with ambiguities, many people take them for granted. But ambiguities taken for granted stop being ambiguities since they cease to attract the attention. If ambiguities are really felt, they are always disruptive.

There are different kinds of disruption, arousing feelings of various intensity. An ironic retort forces awareness on the listener and therefore disrupts his habitual line of thought. A work of art, depending on its profoundness, might penetrate deeper, making man question traditional values and accepted norms. But the ambiguous in nature or in existence might push man further, towards a major breaking point where he sheds his habitual beliefs and life style, resulting in a religious conversion.

What is characteristic of ambiguity is its striking nature. It always implies the presence of an external agent standing outside one's consciousness and disrupting its habitual flow. Struck by ambiguity, we feel a *presence* of someone or something outside our minds. Behind the ironies and the paradoxes we sense the presence of their author. Behind the ambiguous gaze cast on us we experience, as Sartre described, the presence of the *other*. Similarly, behind the mysterious and ambiguous in nature, man has repeatedly assumed the existence of a transcendental presence. Traditionally, this presence has been viewed as sacred and the place in which it has appeared has been regarded as holy. In all religions, Eliade shows, the sacred has been experienced as disrupting the homogeneity of ordinary space and the routine of ordinary time.[17] For example, the Bible tells us that the angel of the Lord appeared to Moses when the latter saw a burning bush that was not consumed by the fire. Being unusual, ambiguous and disruptive of the normal course of existence, the sacred in all religions arouses feelings which are a mixture of terror and attraction, fear and love, horror and fascination.[18]

But most important, this striking quality of ambiguity, this outside presence that forces itself on our minds, always constitutes a new beginning in cognition or a new point of reference. Confronted by an overwhelming sense of ambiguity or by a prolonged crisis in his life, man may undergo a religious conversion and start a new life. But in much lesser degrees, ambiguities residing in art, irony or humor, may also cause a cognitive "conversion." Ambiguous communication launches the mind on a romantic exploration of new possibilities of existence or new facets of reality. But then the classic tendency of man intervenes and eventually reorganizes his cognition of the world he sees in a new framework and baptizes it with a new *name* or identity.

We can see this cognitive process occurring not only in religious conversions but, although on a much smaller scale, also in the experience aroused by a simple ironic retort. As a result of the ironic retort we analyzed earlier the listener might abandon his previous conviction concerning how wise his friend was and become aware of various shades of wisdom. Obviously, this process is not interminable since the classic tendency of the mind may soon intervene and the listener may eventually decide what wisdom would mean to him and how wise his friend is. He would thereby determine a new identity for the person he knows in the light of the wider awareness of wisdom he has just acquired. In a similar way, once the awe-inspiring ambiguity of the sacred is experienced, a new faith is born in the heart of the believer, a new religion with a new outlook on the world is formed. Ambiguity, whether encountered in ordinary communication, art or natural phenomena, always sets off a process in the mind by which old cognitive structures are shaken. But once the thrust of the ambiguous is felt, a new and wider identity awareness of objects, of people or of the world, starts to crystallize.

Now to make his patient renounce mistaken convictions or rigid *names,* the therapist must develop a sense for this artistic ambiguity which subtly combines a "yes" and a "no." He cannot flatly reject the patient's beliefs but he can soften them and make it easier for the patient to renounce them. Take the paranoid patient whom we mentioned earlier. He claims that the people around him are out to "get" him and he would consider the therapist, too, as "one of them" in case the latter dares to ridicule the paranoic fantasies. Indeed, the therapist avoids confrontation and communicates instead an ambiguous message. He sits near the patient, listens carefully to his words and with a benevolent humor he says: "You know, if *they* don't get you, someone else will; maybe the Communists, the Chinese, the In-

ternal Revenue Service, God. In this world no one wins anyway."
Thus, the therapist does not reject the patient's paranoid ideas and does
not hit him with the truth about their nature. On the contrary, he
ostensibly accepts them, making them part of a wide number of possibilities that are equally or even more menacing. And this is said
while the therapist remains calm and reassuring, seemingly agreeing
with the patient's contentions while reducing them to insignificant
proportions, revealing to the patient how relative his conviction is
in comparision with other possibilities.

Here, then, the goal is not to impose on the patient this or that
"truth" but only to make him renounce a fixed idea, to detach himself
from the finality of a *specific name* and to look out upon a horizon
full of new possibilities. Faced with this exaggerated menace (Chinese,
Communists, etc.,) the patient would eventually form a new identity
awareness of his world or himself. He might perhaps realize that since
he could survive so many dangers he had not even been aware of,
he might also survive his present "enemies." He could, on the other
hand, acquire a deep sense of mortality or philosophical despair so
that he would stop worrying about anyone killing him and thereby
renounce his paranoia altogether. After all, if we all are going to die
anyway, who cares anymore! Or the patient might become more
anxious, seeing now not only his family but the whole world is out to
"get" him. But even in this case, the therapist would achieve his goal
which is that of making his patient *change* his mind, and a mind that
can be changed in one way, can also be later changed in another, more
optimistic direction. What is essential is that the patient himself, not
the therapist, decides to make this change and form a new conviction.

Take the depressed and suicidal patient as another example.
When he expresses his low self-esteem and claims he is unworthy of
love and living, the therapist might earnestly say: "You know, with
the troubles that you have had, many people would become suicidal
and very few would endure them as long as you did." Thus, the
therapist accepts the patient's suicidal thoughts as being normal to
have, given the facts as reported above. However, here the ambiguity
lies in the fact that the therapist accepts the patient's self-deprecations
while tacitly dismissing them; he shows the patient how they actually
constitute a proof of his strength, not his weakness. The therapist
thereby makes the patient realize how the same human condition
might have different values depending on the point of view from which

it is observed. Thus, as with the ironical remark, Mona Lisa's smile and Macbeth's character, the therapist's words and behavior should contain the right measure of ambiguity to help his patient free himself from firmly held convictions and to become aware of a host of new possibilities.

But ambiguity, as we have mentioned, appears in different forms and might produce different effects on the person exposed to it. Interesting in this context is the therapeutic approach recommended by Watzlawick and Haley and is based on what they term "paradoxical communications." Essentially, a paradoxical communication is also an ambiguous combination of an overt agreement and a subtle rejection, an explicit "yes" and an implicit "no." Watzlawick compares it to the philosophy and techniques of judo, where the opponent's thrust is not opposed by a counterthrust, but rather accepted and amplified by yielding to and going with it.[19] The therapist does not oppose but rather feeds into the patient's symptom in an effort to overcome it.

To illustrate, to a couple suffering from the intrusive and overprotective approach of the in-laws, Watzlawick suggested the following. Since the purpose was to stop the husband's parents from treating the couple like children, heaping presents on them as well as telling them what to do, the couple was asked to behave, paradoxically, in an extremely dependent and childlike way. They were to leave their house dirty, their laundry unwashed, neglect the garden, deplete the kitchen of groceries, etc. In other words, they were to call the in-laws and ask them for the same assistance the latter usually liked to offer, only this time the request was to be enormously exaggerated. The result was that the in-laws, after having started to fulfill their traditionally overprotective role and clean the house, cut their visit short and even told the couple that it was time they stopped being so pampered, behaved in an adult fashion and became less dependent on them. Instead of directly opposing the in-laws' overprotective approach, an opposition that had not been successful in the past, the couple managed to achieve their independence in a paradoxical fashion, with the result that the in-laws, instead of overindulging the young couple, now dedicated themselves to the equally gratifying task of weaning them away from dependency.

It follows that in this context, ambiguity, appearing in the form of paradoxical communication, is used to control and change the behavior of others. Of note is the fact that both Haley and Watzlawick first concentrated on the relation between *double bind* patterns of communication and the development of schizophrenic symptoms in people. Drawing on this initial interest in ambiguity expressed in communications among family members, they later became interested in paradoxical communications as means of controlling and changing behavior in people. Haley in particular expands on ambiguity as an expression of power struggle among people as well as being the means to gain control over others. We mentioned earlier his interpretation of psychopathological symptoms as a paradoxical mode of communication designed to manipulate and control people. For example, the wife who would force her husband to stay home while denying that *she* wants it, that is, avoids being personal in her request but instead blames it on her sickness. Haley not only believes that therapists should use the same pattern of paradoxical communication to control the behavior of their patients, but he also tries to show that many existing therapeutic approaches basically consist of the same kind of paradoxical communication.[20]

First he described hypnosis as a typical paradoxical relationship taking place between the hypnotist and his patient. Each side affirms something while denying it. For example, the induction of a hypnotic trance starts with the hypnotist asking his patient to sit down, place his hands on the arms of the chairs and relax. The hypnotist adds: "I don't want you to move your hand, just try to feel it, concentrate on the feeling in your hands." But then the hypnotist proceeds: "In a moment you will feel your hands begin to lift. Lifting, lifting, lifting. . . ." We can put this more directly by paraphrasing; the hypnotist is actually telling the patient: "Relax, don't lift your hand!" and then he adds: "Lift your hand!" To these paradoxical instructions the patient responds in an equally paradoxical manner. He lifts his hand and claims that *he* did not do it, the hand lifted itself by itself or "involuntarily." To take another example, a hypnotist will tell his subject to keep his eyes open and stare at a certain point on the wall. After a while the hypnotist would add: "Your eyelids will close." Again, in response to this "don't close-close" message, the patient will close his eyes and claim *he* did not do it, the eyes closed "involuntarily." Thus the "involuntary" actions of patients in hypnotic trance are basically ambiguous responses to the hypnotist's paradoxical injunctions.

In his book, Haley wants to show that the major psychotherapeutic approaches, from psychoanalysis, behavior modification, to family therapy, are essentially similar in their communicative patterns to hypnotic inductions. Ostensibly, therapists accept the patient's symptom but actually defeat it; they allow patients to continue displaying their symptoms, only this time the symptomatic behavior is under their control and they can therefore stop it. For example, the behavioral psychologist asks his phobic patient to experience his phobias in the office under his instructions and control. If the patient is afraid of snakes, the therapist will ask him to imagine a terrible snake crawling by or that he is playing with a snake, etc. The patient's aroused anxiety becomes then associated with the control of the therapist who can later reduce it through relaxation. Thus, the therapist instructs the patient to experience his phobia yet, at the same time, he manipulates him in such a way as to defeat his anxiety through relaxation. Haley sees the same combination of "yes" and "no" in the communications of psychoanalysts or family therapists with their patients.

Needless to say, Haley's analysis is simplistic in many respects. First, not every symptomatic behavior is a maneuver to control the behavior of another person. In most cases, migraine headaches or depression are simply migraine headaches and depression; they are not messages or "paradoxical communications" addressed to anyone. Second, Haley and Watzlawick are aware of only one impact that ambiguous or paradoxical messages might have, namely the control and defeat of an opponent. We recall that Watzlawick compares paradoxical communications to the techniques of judo which is meant to establish a physical superiority of one person over another. There is absolutely no interest in establishing, either in the patient or in those who are related to his condition, an understanding of a symptom or of the rationale of the therapy being employed in the treatment. In the example mentioned earlier, the therapist's task was to contrive a way to stop the in-laws from intruding in their son's married life. There was no attempt to help the in-laws gain insight concerning their overprotective, dominating behavior and, in general, the development of insight is not the goal of this approach. Emphasis is laid rather on the immediate cessation of an undesired behavior and only those paradoxical injunctions are used that can serve this purpose, making the patient's symptomatic behavior virtually impossible. By deliberately neglecting their house, the young couple forced their in-laws to exceed their habitual "assistance" to the point of exhaustion and self-defeat. Thus, the type of ambiguity Haley or Watzlawick would communicate has a specific goal: to control the patient and extinguish his symptomatic behavior by the elimination of its reinforcing qualities.

Undoubtedly, ambiguity can easily disarm, defeat and control people. An inscrutable look, a mysterious smile, baiting words, unfinished sentences "pregnant" with meaning, the aura of sainthood surrounding a famous soul healer, the magnetic charm that some therapists exude—all these phenomena can easily cast a spell on people, capture their attention and make them suggestible to new ideas or *names*. So a hypnotist can make one believe that a cold object is actually hot, that the painful is actually tolerable or the bitter is sweet. Once a patient is seduced into a suggestible or receptive state of mind, it becomes easy to make him acquire new beliefs. One therapist might suggest to him that "emotional discharge"—loud crying, laughter or uninhibited expressions of all feelings—would be *the* cure for his troubles. Other therapists might suggest a vegetarian diet or the incantation of abracadabra as the key to mental and physical health. Once a therapist learns the magical power of ambiguous communications, he becomes capable of molding the patient's world by directly suggesting to him a new *name* after having destroyed in him an old one. The question is, however, whether Haley's paradoxical communications or any hypnotic suggestion enhances cognitive growth in the patient. The answer is no.

Although cognitive structuring or offering a *name* is the essential part of any therapeutic approach, the patient's acquisition of cognitive resilience is a far more important objective. We mentioned earlier that the Babel therapist not only provides a *name* to his patient but also prepares him to renounce *names*. In this way his approach meets the characteristics of identity awareness and its development in the mind. For a sane identity awareness is not riveted to a single *name* but continues to be constantly in the making. Therefore, the ambiguity that the Babel therapist employs does not aim to control the patient and brainwash him with this or that conviction. In communicating it, the therapist addresses it to himself as well as to his patient. He is not then the "professional" who looks at his patient from above but rather the human being who shares with the patient his weakness in their mutual existential predicaments. Indeed he has *names* to offer to his patients, cognitive structuring as to how they should or should not organize their lives to avoid stress. But along with the confident guidance he offers, the therapist also conveys to his patients that his ideas are neither a magic drug nor an absolutely accurate and scientific truth. He shows them how he often fumbles and gropes for answers, because he is a priest without a specific "church," who acknowledges his limitations.

Let us recall the ambiguous message we mentioned earlier concerning the paranoid patient who claims that his family is out to "get" him. The therapist's answer ("You know, if *they* don't get you, someone else will, etc.") is certainly not a maneuver to gain control over the patient. It is an ambiguous message that accepts the patient's claim yet indirectly rejects it by dwarfing it to an insignificant degree of importance. But the therapist addresses this message to himself as well as to his patient. He wants to remind himself that being a loser is as human as being a winner, that since human beings are mortal, they will be finally overpowered in one way or another. Yet this is no reason to despair, for life still has many possibilities to offer. The essential point to remember is that here the therapist wants to make the patient renounce a fixed idea and develop cognitive resilience or malleability, and it is unlikely to teach him this cognitive resilience and openness if the therapist continuously demonstrates "professional" certitude and unflinching confidence like many of the ancient Sophists. It is like teaching people to become free individuals. One certainly cannot communicate this message to them by harangues or inflamed speeches about freedom. For in this way, they will not learn how to be free but, rather, fanatic or dependent and servile. To teach them freedom one should instead offer them possibilities and let them choose so that they exercise freedom in action and taste its flavor. By the same token, a therapist can help a patient develop cognitive resilience only by being himself a malleable and open person, far removed from the rigid and haughty "class consciousness" that professionalism often develops in people. He always tries to put himself at the same level as his patient.

Thus, when the Babel therapist accepts the ideas of a depressed and suicidal patient by saying: "You know, with the troubles that you have had, many people would have become suicidal and very few would endure them as long as you did," he communicates to him his own conviction that suicidal thoughts are not abnormal and that he, the therapist, could have been in the patient's position. What is essential in this case is that the patient remain puzzled as to the quality of his condition. Perhaps he is not that weak and lowly after all! Doesn't the fact that he is still alive show some degree of endurance? So why not try to go on living? And in the case of the paranoid patient, the therapist's ambiguous remark reminds him that besides his family out to "get" him, life offers other calamities from which he has thus far been saved, so why lose hope? The therapist does not impose any conviction on the patient but only offers him a wide horizon of possibilities from which the patient himself will choose the one he wants. When provided generously, these kinds of ambiguous messages will teach the patient that one can look at life from different angles, that identities are not eternally fixed entities.

Naturally the reader might wonder how one could engender this kind of ambiguity addressed to so many rigid ideas that patients might have. And, indeed, it is not easy to create an ambiguous message appropriate for a specific idea, or is it easy to predict its exact effect. We saw that some ambiguous messages may completely confuse and shatter the mind schizophrenicly. Some messages may hypnotize; some serve to inhibit behavior; some to seduce and to subjugate. Other ambiguities indeed may induce the mind to renounce a rigid conviction which will be replaced, at least for a brief time, with several possibilities. It is the latter type of ambiguity which is needed to establish resilience in people's minds. But how could one create this kind of ambiguity all the time?

This question is closely related to another, equally difficult question. The Babel therapist does not only communicate ambiguous messages to his patients but also counsels them as to how they can improve their situation. How does he know the right counsel to give? Can't he give wrong advice and mislead his patient?

Indeed, while counseling his patients as well as when he communicates ambiguous messages, the therapist is constantly walking on a tightrope. In order to give his patient the right advice, he must be familiar with the latter's cultural background and capable of putting himself in the patient's shoes. On the other hand, to teach the patient cognitive resilience, the therapist must be himself well-trained in life's ambiguities. This means that he cannot isolate himself in academic ivory towers or speak to his patients *ex cathedra*. Like Socrates who pursued knowledge and wisdom in the streets and public markets of Athens, the therapist must be involved in life and always curious to explore its hidden nooks and crannies. And again like Socrates, he should consider self-knowledge the most important knowledge.

Earlier we mentioned the people of Sodom and Gomorrah as an example of rigid identities and a life style that eventually perished. Lot's wife could not leave the burning city without looking backward and she perished too. But Lot could leave the city and begin a new life. However, at the beginning he, too, hesitated and could have died were it not for the angels who kindly took his hand and led him outside the city. In many respects, this is the role of the therapist who has to help his patients renounce an established, yet painful existence and build a new one. And he can successfully accomplish this task only to the extent that he himself is resilient enough to renounce established norms and renew himself constantly. He is unlikely to help his patients if he himself tends to be rigid. This is where Socratic self-knowledge and self-criticism can help the therapist acquire resilience so that he can communicate it to his patients. He should realize that he, like any other person, is only a sojourner on this earth, that the roles one plays in life are temporary Towers where identity persists for a while only to renew itself in other forms.

The therapist requires a thorough knowledge about the patient's cultural background, as well as his own rich experience of life, to counsel people or provide them with *names*. This knowledge is equally essential to the creation of ambiguous messages which expand the patient's consciousness with new viable possibilities. In order to effectively touch the patient's heart and mind, an ambiguous message must be cognitively and culturally relevant. Now if the therapist learns to examine himself constantly in the light of the knowledge he acquires about others, if he does not only observe but also participates in life, his remarks will spontaneously reflect both determination and resilience, conviction and openness. His messages will then resemble works of art which, like Macbeth's character or Mona Lisa's smile, on the one hand show us something definite and on the other hand tell us that much is still hidden behind what is actually shown. It is this sense of open-endedness or cognitive resilience which the Babel therapist tries to develop in himself as well as in his patient.

This is different from many contemporary therapists who like to identify themselves as "professionals" or "scientists" belonging to "churches" with various, eye-catching *names*. "Behavior modification," "assertive therapy," "encounter group therapy," "primal scream" and so on, *ad infinitum*. We saw that in one respect all therapies can be helpful; they all give *names* or explanations with which patients can understand their condition or organize their world. But the crucial test for any therapy would be whether it develops cognitive resilience or fanatic convictions in the patient.

Experienced therapists, regardless of the professional "church" they adhere to, know that the individual patient they see has an elusive identity, differing in one way or another from the general theory they learned about human nature. And it is when a therapist has long trained himself in this elusiveness of identities that he comes to resemble the Babel therapist.

To sum up, a Babel therapist has no definite identity. Like the people of the Bible, he strives to acquire a *name* yet avoids fixed ones. He knows that sane identities always remain in the making. His patients ask him "Why," "What," and "How" in order to find the cause of their troubles, their meaning as well as their cure. He responds by providing them with *names* and definitions so that they may overcome their bewilderment and restructure their cognition. We said that one part of therapy always involves processes of identity-formation in which the causes as well as the antidotes for symptoms are stated. But since mental difficulties always relate to concrete life situations, the therapist will have to answer the patient's questions about the right way to behave or the right action to take. He cannot avoid the important role of giving, hopefully, good advice. This would necessitate a wide knowledge of the patient's cultural background. But above all, the therapist's aim is to make his patient receptive to the renunciation of fixed ideas, widening his cognitive horizons with the awareness of new and viable possibilities. Altogether, the therapist's credentials should include, besides familiarity with the patient's cultural background, a profound knowledge of human culture in general.

It is the role of the therapist to show his patient how to relinquish an established, inflexible existence and to build a new one. He can accomplish this task successfully only to the extent that he himself possesses the resilience he is attempting to create in his patient. This means he has to slough off all traces of professional class consciousness, recognizing his own frailties and limitations. In conveying to his patient the elusiveness of all identities, of their romantic and classic nature, the Babel therapist also provides him with a model of a sane mind which is, symbolically, a half-accomplished and half-destroyed Tower. An old Hebrew proverb goes: "Time is short, there is a lot to do, but it is not up to you to finish the work." Which is to say that a sane identity is a process which has neither an end nor a single, ultimate direction.

Notes

INTRODUCTION

1 Plato's *Protagoras,* 318, 328. In Jowett, B. (Tr.) *The Dialogues of Plato,* New York, Random House, 1937.

2 See Versényi, L., *Socratic Humanism,* New Haven, Yale University Press, 1963.

CHAPTER 1

1 Bleibtreu, J. N., *The Parable of The Beast,* New York, The Macmillan Company, 1968, p. 216-219.

2 Werner, H., The Concept of Development from a Comparative and Organismic Point of View. In D. Harris (Ed.), *The Concept of Development. An Issue in the Study of Human Behavior,* Minneapolis, University of Minnesota Press, 1957.

3 See Flavell, J. H., *The Developmental Psychology of Jean Piaget,* Princeton, Van Nostrand, 1963.

4 Bandura, A., *Aggression—A Social Learning Analysis,* Englewood Cliffs, New Jersey, Prentice-Hall, 1973.

5 See Eibl-Eibesfeldt, I., *Ethology: The Biology of Behavior,* New York, Holt, Rinehart and Winston, 1970, p. 326-334.

6 Lorenz, K., *On Aggression,* New York, Harcourt Brace Jovanovich, 1966.

7 Storr, A., *Human Aggression,* New York, Atheneum, 1968.

8 Eibl-Eibesfeldt, I., *Ethology: The Biology of Behavior,* New York, Holt, Rinehart and Winston, 1970, p. 428-431.

9 Ibid., p. 430.

10 Talmon, J. L., *The Origins of Totalitarian Democracy,* New York, Praeger, 1960.

CHAPTER 2

1 See Flavell, J. H., *The Developmental Psychology of Jean Piaget,* Princeton, Van Nostrand, 1963, p. 41-84.

2 Piaget, J., *The Construction of Reality in the Child,* New York, Basic Books, 1954, p. 36-37.

3   See Newton, E., *The Romantic Rebellion,* New York, Schocken Books, 1964, p. 22-40.

4   See Panofsky, E., *Meaning in the Visual* Arts, Garden City, New York, Doubleday, Anchor Books, 1955.

5   See Habasque, G., *Cubism: Biographical and Critical Study,* New York, Skira 1959.

6   Pascal. B., *Pensées,* (Ed.) Louis Lafuma, London, Everyman's Library, 1960, p. 37.

7   See Mischel, W., *Personality and Assessment,* New York, John Wiley and Sons, 1968.

CHAPTER 3

1   Toulmin, S., *Foresight and Understanding: An Inquiry into the Aims of Science,* Bloomington, Indiana University Press, 1966, p. 99.

2   Eliade, M., *The Myth of the Eternal Return, or Cosmos and History.* Princeton, Princeton University Press/Bollingen, 1971.

3   Eliade, M., *The Sacred and The Profane: The Nature of Religion,* New York, Harper and Row, Publishers, 1961.

4   Lovejoy, A. O., *The Great Chain of Being: The Study of the History of an Idea,* Cambridge, Mass., Harvard University Press, 1948, p. 59.

5   See Pollard, S., *The Idea of Progress: History and Society,* Harmondsworth, Penguin Books, 1971.

6   Eliade, M., *The Sacred and The Profane: The Nature of Religion,* New York, Harper and Row, Publishers, 1961, p. 36.

7   Ibid., p. 29.

8   Ibid., p. 49.

9   Lovejoy, A. O., *The Great Chain of Being: The Study of the History of an Idea,* Cambridge, Mass., Harvard University Press, 1948, p. 288.

10   Toulmin, S., The Alexandrian Trap, Thoughts on "The Eternal Scientist." In *Encounter,* Vol. XLII, no. 1, Jan. 1974, p. 64.

11   Kuhn, T. S., *The Structure of Scientific Revolutions,* 2nd edition, Chicago, The University of Chicago Press, 1970.

12   O'Dea, T. F., *The Sociology of Religion,* New Jersey, Prentice-Hall, 1966.

13   See Koyré, A., *From the Closed World to the Infinite Universe,* Baltimore, The Johns Hopkins University Press, 1957, p. 206-220.

14   Kuhn, T. S., *The Structure of Scientific Revolutions,* 2nd edition, Chicago, The University of Chicago Press, 1970, p. 92-94; 155-159.

15   Weber, M., *The Theory of Social and Economic Organizations,* New York, Oxford University Press, 1947.

16   O'Dea, T. F., *The Sociology of Religion,* New Jersey, Prentice-Hall, 1966, p. 22-23.

17   Ibid., p. 72-97.

18   See Radcliffe-Brown, A. R., *Taboo,* Cambridge, Cambridge University Press, 1938.

19 Bergson, H. L., *The Two Sources of Morality and Religion,* New York, H. Holt and Co., 1935.

20 See Shmueli, A., *Kierkegaard and Consciousness,* Princeton, Princeton University Press, 1971.

21 O'Dea, T. F., *The Sociology of Religion,* New Jersey, Prentice-Hall, 1966, p. 27.

22 See Lovejoy, A. O., *The Great Chain of Being: A Study of the History of an Idea,* Cambridge, Harvard University Press, 1943, p. 42.

23 See Armstrong, A. H., *Plotinus,* London, Allen and Unwin, 1953.

24 Freud, S., Beyond The Pleasure Principle. In *The Standard Edition,* Vol. 18, London, Hogarth Press, 1955.

25 See Zubek, J. P., (Ed.) *Sensory Deprivation: Fifteen Years of Research,* New York, Appleton-Century-Crofts, 1969.

26 See Cofer, C. N., Motivation. In *Annual Review of Psychology,* 1959, 10, 173-202.

27 Harlow, H. F., Motivation as a Factor in the Acquisition of New Responses. In Levine, D. (Ed.) *Current Theory and Research in Motivation: A Symposium,* Lincoln, Nebraska, Nebraska University Press, 1953, p. 24-49.

28 Olds, J. and Milner P., Positive Reinforcement Produced by Electrical Stimulation of Septal Area and Other Regions of Rat Brain. In *Journal of Comparative Physiological Psychology,* 1954, 47, 419-427.

29 See Mussen, P. H., Conger, J. J., and Kagan, J., *Child Development and Personality,* New York, Harper and Row, Publishers, 1956, p. 159.

30 See Berlyne, D. E., *Aesthetics and Psychobiology,* New York, Appleton-Century-Crofts, 1971, p. 75-96.

31 Piaget, J., *Play, Dreams and Imitation in Childhood,* New York, Norton, 1951.

32 Ellis, M. J., *Why People Play,* Englewood Cliffs, New Jersey, Prentice-Hall, 1973, p. 110.

33 See Miller, R. D., *Schiller and The Ideal of Freedom,* Oxford, Clarendon Press, 1970.

CHAPTER 4

1 Szasz, T. S., The Myth of Mental Illness, *American Psychologist,* 1960, 15, 113-118.

2 Eysenck, H. J., *The Biological Basis of Personality,* Springfield, Ill., Thomas, 1967.

3 Mowrer, O. H., "Sin," The Lesser of Two Evils, *American Psychologist,* 1960, 15, 113-118.

4 See Rosenthal, D., *Genetic Theory and Abnormal Behavior,* New York, McGraw-Hill, 1970.

5 Mischel, W., *Personality and Assessment,* John Wiley and Sons, 1968.

6   Bergson, H. L., *Laughter,* In Sypher, W., *Comedy,* New York, Double-day Anchor Books, 1956.

7   Berlyne, D. E., *Aesthetics and Psychobiology,* New York, Appleton-Century-Crofts, 1971.

8   Sartre, J. P., *Being and Nothingness,* New York, Wáshington Square Press, 1966, p. 340-400.

9   Bateson, G., Jackson, D. D., Haley, J., and Weakland, J. H., Toward a Theory of Schizophrenia. In *Behavior Science,* 1956, 1, 251-264.

10 Wynne, L. C., The Injection and the Concealment of Meaning in the Family Relationships and Psychotherapy of Schizophrenics. In Cancro, R. (Ed.) *Schizophrenic Syndrome,* Vol. 3, 1973, p. 443-444.

11 Haley, J., *Strategies of Psychotherapy,* New York, Grune and Stratton, 1963.

12 See Lidz, T., *The Origin and Treatment of Schizophrenic Disorders,* New York, Basic Books, 1973.

13 Payne, R. W., Caird, W. K., and Laverty, S. G., Overinclusive Thinking in Schizophrenia. In Sahakian W. S. (Ed.) *Psychopathology Today,* Itasca, F. E. Peacock Publishers, 1970, p. 277-282.

14 Buss, A. H., and Lang, P. J. Psychological Deficit in Schizophrenia. In Sahakian, W. S. (Ed.) *Psychopathology Today,* Itasca, F. E. Peacock Publishers, 1970, p. 282-295.

CHAPTER 5

1   Lorenz, K., *On Aggression,* New York, Harcourt Brace Jovanovich, 1966.

2   Montagu, M. F. A. (Ed.), *Man and Aggression,* New York, Oxford University Press, 1968.

3   See Bandura, A., *Aggression— A Social Learning Analysis,* Englewood Cliffs, New Jersey, Prentice-Hall, 1973.

CHAPTER 6

1   Freud, S., Analysis Terminable and Interminable. In *The Standard Edition,* Vol. 23, London, Hogarth Press, 1964.

2   See Zax, M., and Cowen, E. L., *Abnormal Psychology: Changing Concepts,* New York, Holt, Rinehart and Winston, 1972.

3   Mischel, W., Toward a Cognitive Social Learning Reconceptualization of Personality. *Psychological Review,* 1973, 80, 252-283.

4   Schachter, S. and Singer, J. E., Cognitive, Social and Physiological Determinants of Emotional State. *Psychological Review,* 1969, 379-399.

5   Valins, S., Cognitive Effects of False Hearth-Rate Feedback. *Journal of Personality and Social Psychology,* 1966, Vol. 4, no.4, 400-408.

6   See Lazarus, R. S., *Psychological Stress and the Coping Process,* New York, McGraw-Hill, 1966.

7   Davison, G. C., Differential Relaxation and Cognitive Restructuring in Therapy with a 'Paranoid Schizophrenic' or 'Paranoid State.' *Proceedings of the American Psychological Association,* 1966, 177-178.

8   Frank, J. D., *Persuasion and Healing, A Comparative Study of Psychotherapy,* Baltimore, The Johns Hopkins University Press, 1961.

9   On the role of cognitive factors in behavior modification see Kanfer, F. H., and Phillips, J. S., *Learning Foundations of Behavior Therapy,* New York, Wiley and Sons, 1970, p. 407-454. See also Locke, E. A., Is "Behavior Therapy" Behavioristic? *Psychological Bulletin,* 1971, 76, 318-327.

10 On the role of suggestion in biofeedback techniques as well as in Transcendental Meditation see Miller, N. E., Barber, T. X., DiCara, L. V., Kamiya, J., Shapiro, D., and Stoyva, J. *Biofeedback and Self-Control,* Chicago, Aldine Publishing Co., 1974, Ch. IX.

11 Truax, C. B., Reinforcement and Non-Reinforcement in Rogerian Psychotherapy. *Journal of Abnormal Psychology,* 1966, 71, 1-9.

12 See Valins, S., and Nisbett, R. E., Attribution Process in the Development and Treatment of Emotional Disorders. In Jones, E. E., Kanouse, D. E., Kelley, H. H., Nisbett, R. E., Valins, S., and Weiner, B. *Attribution: Perceiving the Causes of Behavior,* New York, General Learning Press, 1971.

13 Premack, D., Reinforcement Theory. In Levine, D. (Ed.) *Nebraska Symposium on Motivation,* Lincoln, University of Nebraska Press, 1965.

14 See Versényi, L., *Heidegger, Being and Truth,* New Haven, Yale University Press, 1965.

15 See Shmueli, A., *Kierkegaard and Consciousness,* Princeton, Princeton University Press, 1971.

16 Kierkegaard, S. *The Concept of Irony,* New York, Harper and Row, 1966.

17 Eliade, M., *The Sacred and The Profane: The Nature of Religion,* New York, Harper and Row, 1961, p. 20-113.

18 See O'Dea, T. F., *The Sociology of Religion,* New Jersey, Prentice-Hall, 1966, p. 22-23.

19 Watzlawick, P., Weakland, J., and Fish, R., *Change, Principles of Problem Formation and Problem Resolution,* New York, Norton, 1974.

20 Haley, J., *Strategies of Psychotherapy,* New York, Grune and Stratton, 1963.

Index